LOVE & SERVE

LIVING INTERDEPENDENTLY

Love & Serve: Living Interdependently

Devoted: Discipleship Training for Small Groups

Copyright © 2019 by Clear Creek Community Church and Greg Poore

Editorial Team: Mandy Turner, Ryan Lehtinen, Jon Coffey

Published by Clear Creek Resources

A Ministry of Clear Creek Community Church

999 North FM 270

League City, Texas 77573

ISBN: 978-0-9979469-4-9

All rights reserved. No part of this publication may be reproduced, stored in a retrieval system or transmitted in any form by any means, electronic, mechanical, photocopy, recording or otherwise, without the prior permission of the publisher, except as provided by USA copyright law.

Unless otherwise indicated, all Scripture quotations are taken from:

The Holy Bible: English Standard Version, copyright © 2001 by Crossway Bibles, a division of Good News Publishers. Used by permission. All rights reserved.

All Scripture emphases have been added by the authors.

Printed in the United States of America

CONTENTS

Introduction — 5

Using the Study — 7

Week 1: Transformation Required — 9

Week 2: The Ingredients of Transformation — 37

Week 3: Relationship Requires Truth — 59

Week 4: Walk In the Light — 85

Week 5: Change Begins In the Heart — 109

Week 6: Pray for One Another — 133

Week 7: Include Everyone — 157

Week 8: Be Considerate — 185

Week 9: Share With Each Other — 211

Week 10: Bound By Grace — 237

INTRODUCTION

Since its founding, Clear Creek Community Church has had one mission: to lead unchurched people to become fully devoted followers of Jesus. This mission is simply a modern restating of Jesus' words in Matthew 28:19-20 whereby he commissioned his followers to "make disciples" of the world around them. In essence, Christ shows us what a Christian is to be—a disciple who makes disciples. This is the purpose behind our three-year discipleship process which seeks to train others into becoming a disciple-making disciple. It is based upon the gospel truths explained via the Spiritual Growth Grid:

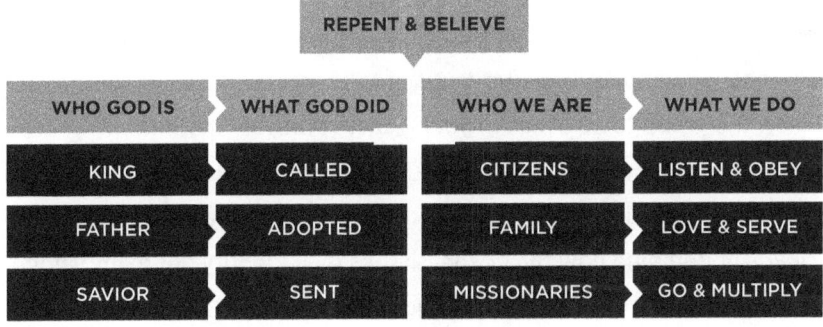

This specific material concerns the second gospel storyline. Participants will learn that, for followers of Jesus, loving and serving each other is a natural response to our gratitude to God for adopting us into his family. As we love the other people he has adopted as much as we love ourselves we worship God by reflecting his love for his children. There are far reaching practical implications to all of this.

- We must *repent* of the thinking and behaviors that keep us separated and independent from other followers of Jesus and we must *believe* God's design for his people is perfect.

- We must *repent* of thinking we or other followers of Jesus, are unworthy to be part of God's family and *believe* God has adopted us to be his children in love and grace.

- We must *repent* of our unwillingness to be known by other people we must *believe* God places us in his family so we can help each other grow up in him.

All of these teachings will be tethered to the gospel storyline that God is a Father who, in the gospel, adopts us as a family who love and serve!

Members can make the most of their small group experience by growing in their gospel fluency whereby identity informs activity. There will likely be opportunities throughout the study to repent from bad beliefs or behaviors and believe the truth of who believers are in the gospel. Allow the group to be a part of your growth process. Share where you are encouraged, rebuked, or challenged to grow as a missionary who goes and multiplies? The aim of this study isn't merely for participants to more clearly understand how the gospel shapes their identity but to implement the activities associated with that identity. May the Lord use this in his grace to make us disciple-making disciples who, as missionaries, share the gospel in word and deed.

Grace to you,
The Elders of Clear Creek Community Church

USING THE STUDY

Devoted is a two-year small group study series focused on training in the essentials of being a disciple who makes disciples. It is designed to help small groups grow deeper in the concepts of the Spiritual Growth Grid. This means, regardless of where you are on the spiritual journey, you play your part in the group each week when you:

Step 1: Memorize the Scripture
Throughout the study you will memorize key Bible passages specifically chosen for the topic. Practice reciting these each day. Try to fill in the blank spaces from memory as you prepare to recite the passages at your next small group meeting.

Step 2: Study the Scripture
The Bible passages are chosen because of the study's general theme. They are good Scriptures to know as either citizens, family, or missionaries. They don't necessarily relate directly to the day's teaching. This is a section where we want disciples to grow in the skill of observing and interpreting a text. The teaching that follows will deal with biblical application.

Step 3: Read the Teaching
Take your time to read through the day's teaching. The questions that follow are designed to help you better process the lesson in light of the Spiritual Growth Grid and apply the principles. Afterwards, take time to

pray using the prompts provided.

Step 4: Do the Weekly Exercise

You will find a weekly exercise at the end of each week's Day 3 material. The exercises often employ different learning styles to practice the principles been taught. Be sure to not only do the exercise but the reflection section as well. The exercises are intended to help build your skill set as a disciple-making disciple.

Step 5: Ready Yourself for Group

The last section of each week's material concludes with the *Get Ready for Group* section. This allows you to summarize your key takeaways for the week in preparation for small group discussion. Please be sure to answer the final question concerning how the week's lessons help you better integrate the Spiritual Growth Grid. This will help your Navigator identify possible areas of further study in order to better live out one's gospel identity. Remember, the point is to be trained to be a disciple who makes disciples!

01

TRANSFORMATION REQUIRED

SCRIPTURE MEMORY

Let the word of Christ dwell in you richly, teaching and admonishing one another in all wisdom, singing psalms and hymns and spiritual songs, with thankfulness in your hearts to God.

—*Colossians 3:16*

LIVING **INTERDEPENDENTLY**

DAY
1

KILLING RELATIONSHIP KILLERS

Scripture Study

COLOSSIANS 3:1-17

If then you have been raised with Christ, seek the things that are above, where Christ is, seated at the right hand of God. ² Set your minds on things that are above, not on things that are on earth. ³ For you have died, and your life is hidden with Christ in God. ⁴ When Christ who is your life appears, then you also will appear with him in glory.

⁵ Put to death therefore what is earthly in you: sexual immorality, impurity, passion, evil desire, and covetousness, which is idolatry. ⁶ On account of these the wrath of God is coming. ⁷ In these you too once walked, when you were living in them. ⁸ But now you must put them all away: anger, wrath, malice, slander, and obscene talk from your mouth. ⁹ Do not lie to one another, seeing that you have put off the old self with its practices ¹⁰ and have put on the new self, which is being renewed in knowledge after the image of its creator. ¹¹ Here there is not Greek and Jew, circumcised and uncircumcised, barbarian, Scythian, slave, free; but Christ is all, and in all.

WEEK 1: TRANSFORMATION REQUIRED

[12] Put on then, as God's chosen ones, holy and beloved, compassionate hearts, kindness, humility, meekness, and patience, [13] bearing with one another and, if one has a complaint against another, forgiving each other; as the Lord has forgiven you, so you also must forgive. [14] And above all these put on love, which binds everything together in perfect harmony. [15] And let the peace of Christ rule in your hearts, to which indeed you were called in one body. And be thankful. [16] Let the word of Christ dwell in you richly, teaching and admonishing one another in all wisdom, singing psalms and hymns and spiritual songs, with thankfulness in your hearts to God. [17] And whatever you do, in word or deed, do everything in the name of the Lord Jesus, giving thanks to God the Father through him.

Observing the Text

Paul begins with a rhetorical question; he asks, "if then you have been raised with Christ," not to question the Colossian's faith but to focus it on the source of true spiritual growth and maturity (v 1-4). Where should we focus our faith?

_____

_____

_____

As Christians, what specific things are we to "put to death" . 5-8)?

_____

_____

_____

What does verse 11 teach about those "who have been raised" with Christ?

_____

_____

_____

Interpreting the Text

What does Paul mean when he says "one has died for all, therefore all have died" but then "he died for all, that those who live might no longer live for themselves..."? How can we "all have died" but there are still "those who live"?

_____

_____

_____

What does it mean to be "in Christ"? What might that look like?

_____

_____

_____

Why does Paul use the phrase "a new creation" to describe those who are in Christ?

_____

_____

_____

Teaching

The family is a gracious gift of God. Within the nurturing bounds of a healthy family, a child learns love, discipline, and responsibility. As their family provides a safe and stimulating environment, children will grow to maturity. The same is true of God's family, the church.

In the first three verses of Colossians 3, Paul underscores the implications of our identity as followers of Jesus. As believers, we have died and been raised with Christ. Our former identity is no longer even visible — our lives are "hidden with Christ in God"! Sounds very similar to what he wrote to the Galatians:

> *"I have been crucified with Christ. It is no longer I who live, but Christ who lives in me. And the life I now live in the flesh I live by faith in the Son of God, who loved me and gave himself for me."*
> —Galatians 2:20

Our identity has changed, transformed by our encounter with Christ. Because we are new people, we shouldn't live the same old lives. Paul instructs us to focus our hearts on the foundation of our new identity and the one true source of life change.

Paul's point is clear. As followers of Jesus we are to be and become people whose lives are living reflections of Jesus. Just as the family is the environment God established for a child to grow and become a mature adult, the family of the church is the essential environment God established to encourage and shape every believer's transformation.

In verses 5-10 of Colossians 3, Paul writes two different lists identifying behaviors and characteristics that must be "put to death" when we are raised with Christ and hidden in him. The first list comprises behaviors that are destructive to our relationship with God. The specific sins mentioned reflect the sexuality and selfishness that dominated the Colossian's culture and represent the practices of those who actively worshipped pagan gods. These practices will not lead us to unity and intimacy with God, they lead to God's wrath.

The second list identifies practices that are destructive to our relationships with people. Paul knows that as members of a family devoted to helping each other grow in Christlikeness, we must "put to death" the behaviors and habits that compromise our relationships with other members of our

LIVING **INTERDEPENDENTLY**

family. A community of God's children must be entirely different from a community of people who do not have faith in Jesus. Consider the definitions of the behaviors Paul says we must put to death:

- Anger: A violent movement; something that boils up suddenly
- Wrath: Long lasting, slow burning anger that one nurses to keep alive
- Malice: A poisoned mind from which evil things are produced
- Slander: Speaking hateful things about someone
- Obscene Talk: Language or speech that is insensitive to the hearer
- Lying: Distorting the truth about ourselves or others

Paul's list summarizes the ways we respond to the actions and personalities of other people when we respond in an "earthly" manner, out of alignment with our new identity. These kinds of responses are deadly to relationships with people, and toxic within the family of the church. Paul leaves no middle ground. For a person raised with and hidden in Christ, a sign of redemption and faith is that you do away with these "relationship killers."

This text teaches us that unity with God produces unity with his people. In Christ, we are to "put off the old self with its practices and... put on the new self, which is being renewed in knowledge after the image of its creator." When we determine to put to death these destructive responses, we both acknowledge God as our true Father and begin to participate in a new community, a new family, where all may grow into maturity.

"If then you have been raised with Christ," kill anger and wrath. Kill malice and slander. Kill obscenity and lying. Put on a new self, reborn and renewed in the image of your creator. Your relationship with God and your relationship with God's children depend on it.

WEEK 1: TRANSFORMATION REQUIRED

Questions for Reflection

Read the definitions of the behaviors Paul says to kill (v 8). Which of those do you know you need to address?

_____
_____
_____

Reflect on how you have seen the negative behaviors listed in verse 8 damage relationships, both your own and others.

_____
_____
_____

What is required for you to "put to death," "put off," and "put away" the destructive behaviors Paul lists as opposed to just minimizing them? What happens if you only minimize destructive behaviors?

_____
_____
_____

Prayer

Pray over some behaviors that you want God to help you "put to death" as a result of reflecting on this text.

SCRIPTURE MEMORY

Let the word of _____ dwell in you richly, teaching and admonishing one another in all wisdom, singing psalms and hymns and spiritual songs, with _____ in your hearts to God.

—*Colossians 3:16*

LIVING **INTERDEPENDENTLY**

DAY
2

THE ENABLERS

Scripture Study

COLOSSIANS 3:1-17

If then you have been raised with Christ, seek the things that are above, where Christ is, seated at the right hand of God. ² Set your minds on things that are above, not on things that are on earth. ³ For you have died, and your life is hidden with Christ in God. ⁴ When Christ who is your life appears, then you also will appear with him in glory.

⁵ Put to death therefore what is earthly in you: sexual immorality, impurity, passion, evil desire, and covetousness, which is idolatry. ⁶ On account of these the wrath of God is coming. ⁷ In these you too once walked, when you were living in them. ⁸ But now you must put them all away: anger, wrath, malice, slander, and obscene talk from your mouth. ⁹ Do not lie to one another, seeing that you have put off the old self with its practices ¹⁰ and have put on the new self, which is being renewed in knowledge after the image of its creator. ¹¹ Here there is not Greek and Jew, circumcised and uncircumcised, barbarian, Scythian, slave, free; but Christ is all, and in all.

¹² Put on then, as God's chosen ones, holy and beloved, compassionate hearts, kindness, humility, meekness, and patience, ¹³ bearing with one

WEEK 1: TRANSFORMATION REQUIRED

another and, if one has a complaint against another, forgiving each other; as the Lord has forgiven you, so you also must forgive. ¹⁴ And above all these put on love, which binds everything together in perfect harmony. ¹⁵ And let the peace of Christ rule in your hearts, to which indeed you were called in one body. And be thankful. ¹⁶ Let the word of Christ dwell in you richly, teaching and admonishing one another in all wisdom, singing psalms and hymns and spiritual songs, with thankfulness in your hearts to God. ¹⁷ And whatever you do, in word or deed, do everything in the name of the Lord Jesus, giving thanks to God the Father through him.

Observing the text

How does Paul describe followers of Jesus? (v. 12)

_____
_____
_____

As Christians what things are we to "let" be characteristic of us? (vs. 15-16)

_____
_____
_____

As Christians what are we to "be"? (v. 15)

_____
_____
_____

As Christians what things are we to "do"? (vs. 15-17)

_____
_____
_____

LIVING **INTERDEPENDENTLY**

Interpreting the text

What do the character qualities in verse 12 have in common?

_____
_____
_____

Why do you think Paul says we should "let the peace of Christ rule" and "let the word of Christ dwell"? Why "let" and not "put on," "be," or "do"?

_____
_____
_____

Verse 15 says we are to "put on" and "let" these character qualities be true of us because we are "one body." Where else in the New Testament is the church described as a body? How do those texts relate to this one? (See Romans 12:3-6; 1 Corinthians 12)

_____
_____
_____

Teaching

In his book *Addiction: A Banquet in the Grave*, author Ed Welch describes a simple conclusion arrived at through research into addictive behaviors: an addict can and will stop being addicted the moment he decides he desires something more than he desires the object of his addiction.

The root of this observation is that there is no void in the human heart. Our hearts will be full. We cannot just remove something from our heart's desires we must replace it. In our text (see verses 5-8; 12-14), Paul describes

WEEK 1: TRANSFORMATION REQUIRED

some relational characteristics of two opposite kinds of people, illustrating how we choose to be one type of person or the other.

To use Paul's imagery in the text, we will "cover ourselves" with something. We will "put on" anger, malice, wrath, and slander, or we will "put on" compassion, kindness, humility, and the like. None of us is completely one way or the other. But, our lives will be characterized by how we usually respond to other people and by what we *usually* do in response to our circumstances. Paul is calling us to glorify God by how we choose to respond to each other. First, he describes relationally destructive behaviors we must "kill," that is, choose not to do (v. 5-9).

Beginning in verse 12, Paul teaches that since we are to live as "one body" who are collectively characterized by our chosen status in God's family, our holiness in Christ, and our security in God's love for us, there are both things we must choose to be and things we must *allow* ourselves to be.

To "put on" is a choice. You decide if you will be compassionate, kind, patient, and forgiving. You make that choice every time you encounter another human being. You make a decision between forgiveness and malice, anger and kindness, slander and humility dozens of times every day. The aggregate of those decisions amounts to your character.

The challenge is that for most of us, most of the time, our response to other people is a default response. We don't make a choice about our response in the specific moment; rather, we bring our response with us before the moment arrives.

How do you enter every encounter with another person with your default response set on love, patience and kindness? First, you let the peace of Christ rule in your hearts (v. 15). That means that you have chosen to believe Jesus is in authority. He has done justice, made provision for you, and given you a life-changing desire for the "things that are above, where Christ is, seated at the right hand of God" (vs. 1-2). It also means that you "let the word of Christ dwell in you richly" (v. 16). You allow the truth and authority of God's word to shape the way you think, the things you desire, and the purpose of your life. You don't seek worldly things, so you don't respond in worldly ways.

Allowing the peace of Christ to rule in us and the Word of Christ to dwell in us enables a transformation of the heart where love, compassion, and kindness win out over anger, malice, and slander. By allowing the peace of Christ to rule in you and the Word of Christ to dwell in you, love, compassion, and kindness can become your default response to other people. You can develop a heart that is ripe for "putting off" old destructive ways and "putting on" the ways of the holy and beloved family of God.

Will you let Christ rule your heart?

Questions for Reflection

What is the relationship between what dwells in and rules your heart and the behaviors that characterize your relationship with other people? (see also Luke 6:43-45)

___

___

___

What would be different about you if the peace of Christ ruled your heart?

___

___

___

WEEK 1: TRANSFORMATION REQUIRED

What would be different about you if the word of Christ dwelt in you *richly*?
_____
_____
_____

Prayer

Ask God to give you a greater desire for the rule of his peace and his Word and help you put on the character of Christ as you interact with other believers.

SCRIPTURE MEMORY

Let the _____ of Christ dwell in you richly, teaching and _____ one another in all wisdom, singing _____ and hymns and spiritual songs, with thankfulness in your hearts to God.

—*Colossians 3:16*

LIVING **INTERDEPENDENTLY**

DAY 3

ROOTED IN THANKFULNESS

Scripture Study

COLOSSIANS 3:1-17

If then you have been raised with Christ, seek the things that are above, where Christ is, seated at the right hand of God. ² Set your minds on things that are above, not on things that are on earth. ³ For you have died, and your life is hidden with Christ in God. ⁴ When Christ who is your life appears, then you also will appear with him in glory.

⁵ Put to death therefore what is earthly in you: sexual immorality, impurity, passion, evil desire, and covetousness, which is idolatry. ⁶ On account of these the wrath of God is coming. ⁷ In these you too once walked, when you were living in them. ⁸ But now you must put them all away: anger, wrath, malice, slander, and obscene talk from your mouth. ⁹ Do not lie to one another, seeing that you have put off the old self with its practices ¹⁰ and have put on the new self, which is being renewed in knowledge after the image of its creator. ¹¹ Here there is not Greek and Jew, circumcised and uncircumcised, barbarian, Scythian, slave, free; but Christ is all, and in all.

WEEK 1: TRANSFORMATION REQUIRED

¹² Put on then, as God's chosen ones, holy and beloved, compassionate hearts, kindness, humility, meekness, and patience, ¹³ bearing with one another and, if one has a complaint against another, forgiving each other; as the Lord has forgiven you, so you also must forgive. ¹⁴ And above all these put on love, which binds everything together in perfect harmony. ¹⁵ And let the peace of Christ rule in your hearts, to which indeed you were called in one body. And be thankful. ¹⁶ Let the word of Christ dwell in you richly, teaching and admonishing one another in all wisdom, singing psalms and hymns and spiritual songs, with thankfulness in your hearts to God. ¹⁷ And whatever you do, in word or deed, do everything in the name of the Lord Jesus, giving thanks to God the Father through him.

Observing the Text

What command does Paul give, in three different ways, in verses 15-17?

What does Paul command we do for each other in verse 16?

How much of what we do as Christians is to be done "in the name of the Lord Jesus"? (v. 17)

Interpreting the Text

What would it look like in practical terms for a person to "do everything in the name of the Lord Jesus"?

LIVING **INTERDEPENDENTLY**

_____
_____
_____

Why does it matter whether you "let the peace of Christ rule in your heart"? What happens if it doesn't?

_____
_____
_____

What are we to be thankful for? How does thankfulness impact the behaviors and character qualities we are to "put to death" and those we are to "put on"?

_____
_____
_____

Teaching

Author Paul Tripp says, "We don't live our lives based on the facts. We live our lives based on our interpretation of the facts."[1] That explains why, for example, one person sitting in a traffic jam is road raging while the person stuck right beside them is happily singing along with the radio. A very good case can be made that our lives are shaped, not so much by what we experience, but by how we respond to what we experience.

In the passage we have been studying, the apostle Paul says "If then you have been raised with Christ...put to death" old earthy behaviors that were self-worshipping and divisive. Instead "put on" the compassion, kindness,

---

[1] Instruments in the Redeemer's Hands; 41

WEEK 1: TRANSFORMATION REQUIRED

and patience that characterize people who are God's chosen children.

But how does God bring about this transformation that changes us from people who respond in anger or slander into people who respond with kindness and patience? What is it within us that shapes the way we respond to circumstances and people? Jesus says in Luke 6:45, "out of the abundance of the heart the mouth speaks."

The previous study noted that this transformation begins when we allow the peace of Christ to rule our hearts and we let the word of Christ dwell in us richly. Paul gives another key in verses 15-17.

- God has chosen you, raised you with Christ, made you holy, called you his beloved and placed you in a new and eternal family! Be thankful! (v. 15)
- Teach and sing and admonish one another with thankfulness! (v. 16)
- Do whatever you do in the name of the Lord Jesus giving thanks to God. (v. 17)

The point is obvious, be thankful!

The changes in character and behavior God calls us to as his children are rooted in and nourished by an abiding and ever-growing thankfulness for what God has done for us through Jesus.

True thankfulness to God reshapes our perspective on everything and everyone. We can sing in the middle of a traffic jam because we know that we deserve death for our sin and we understand we don't deserve the job we're commuting home from, or the car we're driving home in, or the home we're driving to, or the meal we're going to eat when we get there. We have been given immeasurably more than we deserve and could ever quantify!

LIVING **INTERDEPENDENTLY**

Along with the physical provision for life here on earth, we have been given true life, the eternal provision we need for a new life with true purpose. We've been chosen to be his children, we are loved by our Father, and made holy like his Son. Paul would say if you have been raised with Christ, you will be thankful. And, if you are thankful, your gratitude to God in Christ will transform the way you respond to the people God puts in your life.

As we explore how followers of Jesus live interdependently, we are going to dive deep into Colossians 3:15-17. We will see how our thankfulness to God shapes our values, our theology, and our actions. Those three things impact which relationship killers we are willing to "put to death" and whether we will "put on" the characteristics of people who are part of the family of God.

As we reflect on these Scriptures in the coming days, may the Lord give us the faith to be thankful.

Questions for Reflection

What does your response to stress teach you about how thankful you are?
___
___
___

How is the act of worshipping God impacted by how truly thankful a person is?
___
___
___

WEEK 1: TRANSFORMATION REQUIRED

How does true thankfulness help determine which things you are comfortable doing and which things you choose not to do?

_____
_____
_____

Prayer

Thank God today for who he is and what he has done, asking him to open your eyes to his grace and give you a heart of gratitude.

WEEKLY EXERCISE

THE STARTING POINT:
WHAT AM I LIKE TODAY?

Consider each of the following character qualities and score yourself on how accurately each one describes you. Give a high score if it describes you well and a low score if it doesn't. Write one sentence to explain why you give yourself the score you do.

Compassion　1　2　3　4　5　6　7　8　9　10
___
___

Kindness　1　2　3　4　5　6　7　8　9　10
___
___

Humility　1　2　3　4　5　6　7　8　9　10
___
___

Meekness　1　2　3　4　5　6　7　8　9　10
___
___

Patience　1　2　3　4　5　6　7　8　9　10
___
___

Forgiveness　1　2　3　4　5　6　7　8　9　10
___
___

LIVING **INTERDEPENDENTLY**

Get Ready for Group

Write your memorized Scripture.

_____
_____
_____
_____
_____

What observations and interpretations of Scripture were most meaningful to you?

_____
_____
_____
_____
_____

Summarize your key takeaway(s) for this week.

_____
_____
_____
_____
_____

What will you tell the group about the results of your exercise this week?

_____
_____
_____
_____
_____

WEEK 1: TRANSFORMATION REQUIRED

How has this week helped you better understand and apply the Spiritual Growth Grid?

_____
_____
_____
_____
_____

		REPENT & BELIEVE		
WHO GOD IS	WHAT GOD DID		WHO WE ARE	WHAT WE DO
KING	CALLED		CITIZENS	LISTEN & OBEY
FATHER	ADOPTED		FAMILY	LOVE & SERVE
SAVIOR	SENT		MISSIONARIES	GO & MULTIPLY

02

THE INGREDIENTS OF TRANSFORMATION

SCRIPTURE MEMORY

Let the word of Christ dwell in you richly, teaching and admonishing one another in all wisdom, singing psalms and hymns and spiritual songs, with thankfulness in your hearts to God.

—*Colossians 3:16*

LIVING **INTERDEPENDENTLY**

DAY
1

MOVING FROM 'ME' TO 'WE'

Scripture Study

COLOSSIANS 3:15-17

And let the peace of Christ rule in your hearts, to which indeed you were called in one body. And be thankful. [16] Let the word of Christ dwell in you richly, teaching and admonishing one another in all wisdom, singing psalms and hymns and spiritual songs, with thankfulness in your hearts to God. [17] And you do, in word or deed, do everything in the name of the Lord Jesus, giving thanks to God the Father through him.

Observing the Text

Where is the peace of Christ to rule? What do you think that means?

_____
_____
_____

What activities are we called to do as a community (v. 16)?

_____
_____

WEEK 2: THE INGREDIENTS OF TRANSFORMATION

What key themes do you observe in these three verses?

_____
_____
_____

Interpreting the Text

Does this passage describe things we do as individuals or as a community? Why do you think Paul chooses to focus on this?

_____
_____
_____

Why does Paul connect the peace of Christ ruling in your heart to the call to live as one body?

_____
_____
_____

What is the impact of God's word on our relationships and our worship?

_____
_____
_____

Teaching

What does Colossians 3:15-17 teach us? Does the "peace of Christ ruling our hearts" produce thankfulness, or does thankfulness in our hearts produce peace? Does the "word of Christ dwelling in us richly" produce worship rooted in thankfulness, or does thankfulness to God produce worship? Yes, of course, all the above! These verses paint a beautiful picture of how trust in Jesus and submission to God's word create a unique community of people who overflow with thankfulness. At the same time, our thankfulness to God colors everything we do in life and worship, motivating our belief and obedience.

The focus of the calls, challenges, and commands in these verses is to a community, not a single person. When we are adopted by God into his family, we are given responsibility for each other.

You were called to let the peace of Christ rule in you "in one body." That means the relationships we share in the body of Christ, the family of those adopted by God, are to be characterized by the peace of Christ (See a description of these relationships in Philippians 2:1-13). If, as Jesus says in Luke 6:45, "out of the abundance of the heart the mouth speaks," his peace ruling our hearts will enable us to respond to each other with the attributes Paul encourages us to put on in Colossians 3:12-14.

True thankfulness to Jesus means that we respond to the gifts and flaws of our brothers and sisters in Christ through the lens of what Jesus did on the cross to free us from the personal condemnation we rightly deserve for our sin. Just as Christ has loved us, served us and sacrificed for himself for us, so we are to love, serve, and sacrifice for each other as we live together in one body.

But here's the thing: this is a necessarily mutual call to service and sacrifice. No organism can sustain itself if one part denies its role in the body or is in continual rebellion or conflict with the others. When Paul speaks of putting off or on certain attributes, he is calling believers to reject the behaviors that reflect an autonomous spirit, and instead, choose the responsibility and love that come with being part of a family.
This is why Paul's challenges us to "put off" and "put to death" the things listed in Colossians 3:5-10. We must understand we are to be continually

growing in how the gospel transforms the ways we think and live because our personal character profoundly affects all those with whom we live in community. The character we add to the body affects everyone else. In the same way, a gospel-oriented investment in one another—praying, serving, admonishing, encouraging, teaching—will enable us to grow in how we experience life as the body of Christ. And, it isn't a one-way street. When we open our lives and allow others to invest in us, the entire community benefits.

It is thankfulness to Jesus that transforms a person's thinking from self-centered to others-centered. Thankfulness to Jesus enables us to see the sin and immaturity of another person in light of our own. When we do, we can humbly experience repentance and maturity as a physical expression of the grace of God at work. This is what Paul is commanding us to do for each other as we live out our thankfulness in one body.

"And let the peace of Christ rule in your hearts, to which indeed you were called in one body. And be thankful."

Questions for Reflection

If the peace of Christ rules in your heart, how does it determine the way you respond to other people's sin or immaturity?

_____

_____

_____

Do you really see yourself as part of one body as these verses describe? How does this impact your interactions with other believers?

_____

_____

_____

LIVING **INTERDEPENDENTLY**

Think about each person in your group. In what ways does your thankfulness to Jesus shape how you live with them?

_____
_____
_____

Prayer

Thank Jesus today for both who he is and what he has done.

SCRIPTURE MEMORY

Let the _____ dwell in you richly, teaching and admonishing one another _____, singing psalms and hymns and spiritual songs, with thankfulness in your _____ to God.

—Colossians 3:16

LIVING **INTERDEPENDENTLY**

DAY
2

WISDOM AND WORSHIP

Scripture Study

COLOSSIANS 3:15-17

And let the peace of Christ rule in your hearts, to which indeed you were called in one body. And be thankful. [16] Let the word of Christ dwell in you richly, teaching and admonishing one another in all wisdom, singing psalms and hymns and spiritual songs, with thankfulness in your hearts to God. [17] And you do, in word or deed, do everything in the name of the Lord Jesus, giving thanks to God the Father through him.

Observing the text

What are we to do with the word of Christ?

_____
_____
_____

What do the activities we are called to do in verse 16 have in common?

_____
_____
_____

What key response motivates the activities in verse 16?

___

Interpreting the text

What connection is there between the word of Christ and the psalms, hymns, and spiritual songs we are to sing?

___

How does the word of Christ dwell in someone "richly"? What does that look like?

___

What is the difference between "being thankful" (v. 15, 16) and "giving thanks" (v. 17)?

___

Teaching

An important thing to notice about Colossians 3:16 is that Paul connects the "word of Christ" with wisdom. A committed trust and intimacy with the word of Christ is the source of wisdom because the word of Christ is wisdom.

LIVING **INTERDEPENDENTLY**

Wisdom is the understanding of life and the basis of decision-making that proceeds from absolute trust in who Jesus is and what his gospel promises. We are to teach each other about Jesus. We are to come together as his children to reflect on his beauty, glory, and grace and then admonish each other to fully embrace a life of wisdom.

To admonish someone means to counsel them against something, to warn and even to scold when necessary. Paul is commanding us to intervene in each other's lives when it comes to the behaviors we are to "put off" and "put to death." We are to help each other be transformed by the power of the word of Christ at work in us.

What is essential for the body to grow is that the motivation for all teaching and admonition is the mutual spiritual well-being of everyone in the community. We are accountable to the truth and wisdom of the word of Christ, not our personal preferences and sensitivities. This is where we need compassionate hearts, kindness, humility, meekness, and patience! We are to be motivated to engage each other by the gospel, not because we are annoyed. So, the key is to grow in allowing God's word of wisdom to inform the way we respond to each other in all seasons and experiences.

The second thing Paul says in verse 16 is that the word of Christ dwelling in us richly should result in "singing." Singing is a verbal expression of thankfulness. "Psalms and hymns and spiritual songs" engage our emotions as they teach us truths about God and remind us of why we are thankful. Some translations of the Bible render the phrase "with thankfulness in your hearts to God" as "a state of grace." In other words, our songs well up from within us as we embrace and rejoice in what Jesus has done for us. When we sing together, we engage in a fundamental part of the family life of God's children, praising our God and Father publicly. Singing together unifies us as a family as we celebrate God's goodness and our mutual state of grace.

WEEK 2: THE INGREDIENTS OF TRANSFORMATION

It is important to recognize both aspects of what Paul is describing in this verse. There is the challenge, and associated tension, of living together in the kind of relationships where submission to the word of Christ is expected and publicly addressed. There is also the unifying activity of gathering to proclaim our thankfulness and standing in God's grace as a community. Being and becoming a gospel family requires both.

Questions for Reflection

Are you receptive to being admonished for your behavior when it is inconsistent with the word of Christ? What affects your willingness to hear correction from others?

___

___

___

How familiar are you with the word of Christ? Are you continually growing in your intimacy with God's word?

___

___

___

Do you actively participate with the church in singing psalms, hymns, and spiritual songs? How can our singing be a measurement of our thankfulness?

___

___

___

Prayer

Find a Psalm that voices thankfulness to God and pray its words.

SCRIPTURE MEMORY

Let the word of Christ _____ richly, teaching and _____ _____ in all wisdom, singing psalms and hymns and spiritual songs, with thankfulness in your hearts to God.

—*Colossians 3:16*

LIVING **INTERDEPENDENTLY**

DAY
3

RAISED WITH CHRIST

Scripture Study

COLOSSIANS 3:1-17

If then you have been raised with Christ, seek the things that are above, where Christ is, seated at the right hand of God. ² Set your minds on things that are above, not on things that are on earth. ³ For you have died, and your life is hidden with Christ in God. ⁴ When Christ who is your life appears, then you also will appear with him in glory.

⁵ Put to death therefore what is earthly in you: sexual immorality, impurity, passion, evil desire, and covetousness, which is idolatry. ⁶ On account of these the wrath of God is coming. ⁷ In these you too once walked, when you were living in them. ⁸ But now you must put them all away: anger, wrath, malice, slander, and obscene talk from your mouth. ⁹ Do not lie to one another, seeing that you have put off the old self with its practices ¹⁰ and have put on the new self, which is being renewed in knowledge after the image of its creator. ¹¹ Here there is not Greek and Jew, circumcised and uncircumcised, barbarian, Scythian, slave, free; but Christ is all, and in all.

¹² Put on then, as God's chosen ones, holy and beloved, compassionate hearts, kindness, humility, meekness, and patience, ¹³ bearing with one

another and, if one has a complaint against another, forgiving each other; as the Lord has forgiven you, so you also must forgive. [14] And above all these put on love, which binds everything together in perfect harmony. [15] And let the peace of Christ rule in your hearts, to which indeed you were called in one body. And be thankful. [16] Let the word of Christ dwell in you richly, teaching and admonishing one another in all wisdom, singing psalms and hymns and spiritual songs, with thankfulness in your hearts to God. [17] And whatever you do, in word or deed, do everything in the name of the Lord Jesus, giving thanks to God the Father through him.

Observing the Text

Now that we've spent some significant time in this text, what specific things stand out to you?

_____
_____
_____

Interpreting the Text

How do the key teachings in this text instruct us as we learn to live interdependently?

_____
_____
_____

Teaching

As followers of Jesus, we have been given a new identity. We are a family of people adopted by God, who is our gracious Father. Much of the practical instruction given in the New Testament challenges us to put this new identity into action by loving and serving one another. The Colossians text we have studied for the last two weeks is just one place where the Bible addresses the specifics of how we are to live with each other in a way that honors our identity as God's children.

Reflect on the flow of Paul's thinking in Colossians 3:1-17. It begins with Jesus, "If you have been raised with Christ..." Paul is not questioning whether the Colossians have been raised with Christ, but rather, he is calling them to live out the new identity they have received because they *have been* raised with Christ. They are God's children and part of his family. When we join God's family, the purpose of our life dramatically shifts to Jesus and the implications of his gospel for this life and the life to come.

Since we are raised with Christ and have a radical new purpose, we must leave behind the characteristics and behaviors that once dominated our lives before God adopted us in Christ. We "put to death" and "put off" behaviors that are inconsistent with our new identity and are detrimental to the members of our new family. We no longer see each other the same way the world sees people. We are a family for whom "Christ is all, and in all." Our lives are intertwined and interdependent as brothers and sisters in Christ. As we live with each other the way Jesus lives with us, our relationships are refined and God is glorified.

The abiding and sustaining motivation for what we do as a family is *thankfulness*. Thankfulness allows the peace of Christ to dwell in our hearts and steadily grows as we embrace God's word of wisdom and proclaim his grace. Everything we do—every word spoken, every idea developed, every action taken—is done out of thankfulness to Jesus.

We love and serve each other when we put away anger and slander and obscene talk. We love and serve each other when we are kind and humble and patient. We love and serve each other when our thankfulness is evident to all through our wise choices and vigorous praise.

WEEK 2: THE INGREDIENTS OF TRANSFORMATION

Our ongoing struggle to "put off" the attributes of our former life and "put on" the character of Christ really serves to show us areas in our hearts where we have yet to fully embrace our identity as members of God's family. As we work through how we live interdependently over the coming weeks, have the courage to ask yourself the hard questions about where you differ from the character Paul describes in Colossians 3. Ask God to show you where you mistrust his Fatherhood, doubt your adoption, or resist embracing your new family.

You are God's adopted child. Your life is "hidden with Christ"! Believe, embrace, and grow up in this amazing truth!

Questions for Reflection

Which of your beliefs and actions detract from your ability to live as part of a gospel family? What are your struggles with God?

_____
_____
_____

Which of your beliefs and actions contribute to your ability to live as part of a gospel family? What are your strengths?

_____
_____
_____

Prayer

Ask God to show you where you struggle with your identity as part of his family.

WEEKLY EXERCISE

PRAISE IN PUBLIC

Fully participate in the singing at church this week. Before church, pray with thankfulness for Jesus and his church and ask him to open your heart to praise him. As we sing, pay attention to the lyrics and emotional tone of the songs, especially what the songs teach about God.

After church, write down a summary of your experience and share it with your group.

LIVING **INTERDEPENDENTLY**

Get Ready for Group

Write your memorized Scripture.

_____
_____
_____
_____
_____

What observations and interpretations of Scripture were most meaningful to you?

_____
_____
_____
_____
_____

Summarize your key takeaway(s) for this week.

_____
_____
_____
_____
_____

What will you tell the group about the results of your exercise this week?

_____
_____
_____
_____
_____

WEEK 2: THE INGREDIENTS OF TRANSFORMATION

How has this week helped you better understand and apply the Spiritual Growth Grid?

_____
_____
_____
_____
_____

REPENT & BELIEVE

WHO GOD IS	WHAT GOD DID	WHO WE ARE	WHAT WE DO
KING	CALLED	CITIZENS	LISTEN & OBEY
FATHER	ADOPTED	FAMILY	LOVE & SERVE
SAVIOR	SENT	MISSIONARIES	GO & MULTIPLY

03

RELATIONSHIP REQUIRES TRUTH

SCRIPTURE MEMORY

If we confess our sins, he is faithful and just to forgive us our sins and to cleanse us from all unrighteousness.

—1 John 1:9

LIVING **INTERDEPENDENTLY**

DAY
1

TRUSTING GOD TO TELL THE TRUTH

Scripture Study

JOHN 1:14-18

And the Word became flesh and dwelt among us, and we have seen his glory, glory as of the only Son from the Father, full of grace and truth. [15] *(John bore witness about him, and cried out, "This was he of whom I said, 'He who comes after me ranks before me, because he was before me.'")* [16] *For from his fullness we have all received, grace upon grace.* [17] *For the law was given through Moses; grace and truth came through Jesus Christ.* [18] *No one has ever seen God; the only God, who is at the Father's side, he has made him known.*

JOHN 3:16-21

"For God so loved the world, that he gave his only Son, that whoever believes in him should not perish but have eternal life. [17] *For God did not send his Son into the world to condemn the world, but in order that the world might be saved through him.* [18] *Whoever believes in him is not condemned, but whoever does not believe is condemned already, because he has not believed in the name of the only Son of God.* [19] *And this is the*

WEEK 3: RELATIONSHIP REQUIRES TRUTH

judgment: the light has come into the world, and people loved the darkness rather than the light because their works were evil. ²⁰ For everyone who does wicked things hates the light and does not come to the light, lest his works should be exposed. ²¹ But whoever does what is true comes to the light, so that it may be clearly seen that his works have been carried out in God."

Observing the Text

According to these passages, what specific things has Jesus done?

_____
_____
_____

List the names, titles, and descriptions given to Jesus in these texts.

_____
_____
_____

What key themes connect these two texts?

_____
_____
_____

Interpreting the Text

What is the difference between the law brought by Moses and the grace and truth that came through Jesus Christ?

_____
_____
_____

How does the metaphor of "light" help us understand Jesus?

_____

_____

_____

What is a distinguishing characteristic of those who believe in Jesus?

_____

_____

_____

Teaching

There are bicycles, and then there are *bicycles*. You can get a cheap one, and it counts as a real bike, you can pedal it and the tires roll. Or, you can pay a lot more and get an expensive bike that works the same way. What's the difference? Why would someone pay more for what could generally be called "the same thing"? The difference is in what the bikes are made from. The inexpensive one is going to be steel or aluminum, plastic, and low-grade moving parts. The costlier one is going to be carbon fiber or titanium with high-grade, durable moving parts. Have no doubt, if you ride each of the bikes for very long the difference will be obvious.

Relationships are a bit like bicycles. From the outside they can look to be pretty much the same, but if you are in one for very long, you discover that what it's made from makes all the difference. This is true of a relationship with God and of relationships between people.

One key component upon which the quality and durability of every relationship depends is *truth*. It is possible to have a "relationship" without truth, but it will be superficial, short-lived, and filled with bad drama. Living and speaking in truth is the investment you make in a relationship that determines the quality and durability of that relationship. Unfortunately, the truth is that most of us are reluctant to tell the truth about ourselves.

When you read the texts we are studying this week, you can't miss the theme of truth. The glory of Jesus is that he is both grace and truth. As John1:17 says, "Grace and truth came through Jesus Christ."

Jesus is the embodiment of the truth of God: God's power, holiness, and righteousness. Jesus is also the ultimate expression of the mercy, compassion, and love God has for people, revealed to us and paid for by his self-sacrifice.

In John 3:16-21 we are called to make the seemingly impossible journey from darkness into the light of truth. There is no grey area; it is darkness or it is light. It is evil and wickedness or it is truth and life "carried out in God."

In order to enter the light, we must not only confront the truth about ourselves, we must believe that Jesus really did come in both grace and truth. We must really believe "God did not send his Son into the world to condemn the world," but to save us in Christ. If we, the Father's adopted children, are going to live the kind of lives we are called to live in Christ, we must believe that Jesus has swallowed up all of the destructive and humiliating truth about us in *grace*.

You might think your hesitation to walk in the light has to do with what you know to be true of yourself: that you are a sinner and undeserving of God's love, continuing to fail when you should be better by now. But, our hesitation to walk in the light has less to do with what we believe about ourselves and more to do with a failure to believe and trust that God really means it when he says, "Whoever believes in [Jesus] is not condemned." What impedes our spiritual growth, and inhibits our relationship with God, is that we don't truly believe God has atoned for, and removed, the shame and guilt for *all* our sin. We can come up with a billion reasons to hide, but they all boil down to this: we don't really believe what the Father says is true.

Before we can become the kind of family the Father intended to create when he adopted us, we must choose to believe the Father is telling the truth about himself. Before we can love and serve each other, we have to believe that God is telling the truth when it comes to the truth about us, that he has adopted us as his children in spite of our sins.

The moment we choose to embrace who we really are in Christ, we are free to step into the light. We can let the truth and grace of Jesus transform how we think and what we do. Then, we can begin to live together as a family who love and serve each other in ways that truly reflect our identity and God's family.

Questions for Reflection

What happens in relationships between people who don't tell the truth? How do similar things happen in our relationship with God?

_____
_____
_____

What do you think God means when he says "whoever believes in him is not condemned"?

_____
_____
_____

WEEK 3: RELATIONSHIP REQUIRES TRUTH

How is Jesus able to fully embody both truth and grace?

_____
_____
_____

Prayer

Ask God to help you fully believe Jesus' death is all-sufficient to restore your relationship to God the Father.

SCRIPTURE MEMORY

If we confess our ___, he is faithful and just to forgive us our sins and to cleanse us from all _____.

—*1 John 1:9*

LIVING **INTERDEPENDENTLY**

DAY
2

WALKING IN THE LIGHT

Scripture Study

JOHN 3:16-21

"For God so loved the world, that he gave his only Son, that whoever believes in him should not perish but have eternal life. [17] For God did not send his Son into the world to condemn the world, but in order that the world might be saved through him. [18] Whoever believes in him is not condemned, but whoever does not believe is condemned already, because he has not believed in the name of the only Son of God. [19] And this is the judgment: the light has come into the world, and people loved the darkness rather than the light because their works were evil. [20] For everyone who does wicked things hates the light and does not come to the light, lest his works should be exposed. [21] But whoever does what is true comes to the light, so that it may be clearly seen that his works have been carried out in God."

Observing the text

Why did God send his only Son, and for what purpose?

_____

_____

WEEK 3: RELATIONSHIP REQUIRES TRUTH

What separates those who are condemned from those who are not?

_____

_____

_____

Why do people love darkness and hate the light?

_____

_____

_____

Interpreting the text

What do you think John means by the phrase "whoever does what is true comes to the light"?

_____

_____

_____

What do you think are some works that are carried out in God? What is the person doing?

_____

_____

_____

In what specific ways does believing in Jesus change a person?

_____

_____

_____

LIVING **INTERDEPENDENTLY**

Teaching

A member of my small group walked in and sat down one morning and announced that he was getting a divorce, so he would not be able to come to group any more. Then he got up and left. None of us had any idea he had been in the process of a divorce, or that he even had any difficulties in his marriage. This man had been sitting in our group for over a year, and none of us really knew him.

Why are people so reluctant to admit what is really going on in their lives? Why would someone attend a small group for months and never speak of their real day-to-day experiences? How could someone study the Bible with a group of people and never admit where they have questions, struggles, or doubts about what it says? It could be they are embarrassed or afraid the people in the group won't understand or accept their struggles. However, Jesus declares that there is another motivation:

> *And this is the judgment: the light has come into the world, and people loved the darkness rather than the light because their works were evil. For everyone who does wicked things hates the light and does not come to the light, lest his works should be exposed.*
>
> —John 3:19-20

The real reason people can sit in a small group and not talk about what they are really thinking and doing is because they are protecting the things they are doing. People love the darkness—the part of life hidden from people and seemingly from God—because they love their secret choices and experiences more than they love God or other people. It sounds harsh, but it's true. The root of separation from God and people is self-serving, self-love that only shows people what we want them to see and hides the rest of us. We all do it, and we tolerate it from each other because we all know that we all do it.

Jesus describes an alternative: "But whoever does what is true comes to the light" (3:21). It is critical to note that the person John is describing in verse 21 has responded to the invitation of the Gospel to become true and whole in Christ. They have not cleaned up their own lives and made themselves worthy of the light. They have simply believed that Jesus came in *truth and grace*, and the truth about them can be open to the light because they are satisfied that Jesus' grace covers it all, even the not so flattering parts.

Jesus is the light. He is the wisdom of obedience to God the Father, the truth of God's authority, the personification of God's mercy and love, and God's ultimate expression of grace. Jesus is the power of forgiveness and redemption for everyone who will trust him and enter into his light.

Before you can risk being vulnerable and exposed to other people with the truth about yourself, you must trust Jesus with the truth about yourself. You must tell him the truth about yourself and know he has forgiven and redeemed you. When you believe the truth about you is no longer a source of shame but a witness to the truth and grace of Jesus, you are free to "walk in the light."

Do you want to enjoy a small group that really matters in your life? Walk in the light.

LIVING **INTERDEPENDENTLY**

Questions for Reflection

Why do you think people are so reluctant to be open and honest with others about what they've done, what they think, and where they struggle with God?

_____
_____
_____

What do you think when you read John 3:19-20? Do you believe people love darkness rather than light?

_____
_____
_____

How does (or should) trusting Jesus with the truth about yourself enable you to be honest with people?

_____
_____
_____

Prayer

Admit to God the things you have been hiding from him. Ask God to help you fully trust the truth and grace of Jesus.

SCRIPTURE MEMORY

If we _____ our sins, he is _____ and just to _____ us our sins and to cleanse us from all unrighteousness.

—*1 John 1:9*

LIVING **INTERDEPENDENTLY**

DAY
3

A SERIOUS LOOK IN THE MIRROR

Scripture Study

JOHN 3:16-21

"For God so loved the world, that he gave his only Son, that whoever believes in him should not perish but have eternal life. [17] For God did not send his Son into the world to condemn the world, but in order that the world might be saved through him. [18] Whoever believes in him is not condemned, but whoever does not believe is condemned already, because he has not believed in the name of the only Son of God. [19] And this is the judgment: the light has come into the world, and people loved the darkness rather than the light because their works were evil. [20] For everyone who does wicked things hates the light and does not come to the light, lest his works should be exposed. [21] But whoever does what is true comes to the light, so that it may be clearly seen that his works have been carried out in God."

JAMES 1:22-25

But be doers of the word, and not hearers only, deceiving yourselves. For if anyone is a hearer of the word and not a doer, he is like a man who looks *intently at his natural face in a mirror. For he looks at himself and goes away and at once forgets what he was like. But the one who looks into the perfect law, the law of liberty, and perseveres, being no hearer who forgets but a doer who acts, he will be blessed in his doing.*

Observing the Text

What does this text say is the judgment has God made?

How does this text describe *works*, both of those in the darkness and those in the light?

Interpreting the Text

What "work" has God done according to this text?

What makes a work wicked?

How do the metaphors of "hearing" and "seeing" help us understand what it means to respond to God in an appropriate way?

Teaching

James equates looking into a mirror and learning what your face looks like with looking into God's word and learning what your life looks like. It is kind of ridiculous that someone would examine themselves in the mirror and see that their hair is messed up and there is spaghetti sauce on their chin, but then walk away without doing anything to change what they've seen. That would be embarrassing and awkward for everyone. James says the same is true of a person who sits under the teaching of God's word, or reads it for themselves, but then walks away unaffected by it. That doesn't make any sense! James doesn't just say it is embarrassing or potentially offensive, he says it is self-deceiving.

James implies that the reason a person would be a *hearer* but not a *doer* is because they don't believe they need to do anything. They believe they are just fine the way they are, that somehow they have perfectly accomplished Scripture's call to live out the character of Jesus. James says that is obviously not the case; instead, the person is just ignoring the true nature of their heart and character. James calls us to the same challenge that Paul extends in his letter to the Romans:

> *For by the grace given to me I say to everyone among you not to think of himself more highly than he ought to think, but to think with sober judgment, each according to the measure of faith that God has assigned.*
> —Romans 12:3

The picture is of a person who exposes their character—their desires, thoughts, habits, and choices—to the scrutiny of God's word, and then carefully considers every area where there is a difference between their character and the character of Jesus. The questions we must learn to ask ourselves in light of God's word are "Who am I really?" and "Am I living a life worthy of an adopted child of the Heavenly Father?" When we examine the word of God, it becomes evident that the answer to the latter question is "yes" in some ways and "no" in other ways. That is true of everyone. James is urging us to consider the areas of our lives where the answer is "no."

This passage ends with two very encouraging things. The first is that James says the doer of the word *perseveres*. It takes time, energy, and effort to allow God's Spirit to work in, and to transform, your character. James doesn't scold anyone for needing to grow; he scolds the person who ignores their need to grow and puts no effort into it. It is comforting to know growing in Christlikeness takes perseverance. There is no magic involved and no instantaneous way we can change our character. Instead, as God's adopted children we persevere in a life of becoming like our Father.

The second encouraging thing James says is about the law. He says it is the law of *liberty*. There is freedom in being a doer of God's word. There is liberty because there is release from bondage to sinful and destructive ways of thinking and living. There is freedom from the need to hide our true selves from God and people. There is freedom to be imperfect and still completely loved. This liberty in Christ comes as we embrace his perfect law and then grow in how we live it out.

You cannot overestimate the value of serious examination of your own life. As you discuss your struggles, questions, and sin, you invite others to do the same. Your perseverance and growth are part of how God will encourage and transform the people around you.

Be a doer of the word. Look intently in the mirror, see the real you, and refuse to run away.

LIVING **INTERDEPENDENTLY**

Questions for Reflection

What commands that you've read in the Bible do you prefer to just ignore?

_____
_____
_____

Do you believe James's statement that God's perfect law is the law of liberty? If not, what parts feel constraining to you?

_____
_____
_____

Would you say you are persevering in becoming a more devoted follower of Jesus? What are you doing that helps you most?

_____
_____
_____

Prayer

Ask God to show you where your character is not in tune with your identity as his adopted child and how you can grow in that area through faith.

WEEKLY EXERCISE

FINDING GROWTH OPPORTUNITIES

Write down the book, chapter, and verse of three specific teachings of the Bible you struggle to believe, accept, or obey. Write one sentence explaining why, and one sentence explaining how what you believe about God as your Father should impact your response to that text.

1. Book/Chapter/Verse _____

Why I struggle:
_____
_____
_____

If God is the Father:
_____
_____
_____

2. Book/Chapter/Verse _____

Why I struggle:
_____
_____
_____

If God is the Father:
_____
_____
_____

3. Book/Chapter/Verse _____

Why I struggle:
_____
_____
_____

If God is the Father:
_____
_____
_____

LIVING **INTERDEPENDENTLY**

Get Ready for Group

Write your memorized Scripture.

_____
_____
_____
_____
_____

What observations and interpretations of Scripture were most meaningful to you?

_____
_____
_____
_____
_____

Summarize your key takeaway(s) for this week.

_____
_____
_____
_____
_____

What will you tell the group about the results of your exercise this week?

_____
_____
_____
_____
_____

WEEK 3: RELATIONSHIP REQUIRES TRUTH

How has this week helped you better understand and apply the Spiritual Growth Grid?

_____
_____
_____
_____
_____

REPENT & BELIEVE

WHO GOD IS	WHAT GOD DID	WHO WE ARE	WHAT WE DO
KING	CALLED	CITIZENS	LISTEN & OBEY
FATHER	ADOPTED	FAMILY	LOVE & SERVE
SAVIOR	SENT	MISSIONARIES	GO & MULTIPLY

04

WALK IN THE LIGHT

SCRIPTURE MEMORY

If we confess our sins, he is faithful and just to forgive us our sins and to cleanse us from all unrighteousness.

—*1 John 1:9*

LIVING **INTERDEPENDENTLY**

DAY
1

THE BRUTAL FACTS

Scripture Study

1 JOHN 1:5-10

This is the message we have heard from him and proclaim to you, that God is light, and in him is no darkness at all. ⁶ If we say we have fellowship with him while we walk in darkness, we lie and do not practice the truth. ⁷ But if we walk in the light, as he is in the light, we have fellowship with one another, and the blood of Jesus his Son cleanses us from all sin. ⁸ If we say we have no sin, we deceive ourselves, and the truth is not in us. ⁹ If we confess our sins, he is faithful and just to forgive us our sins and to cleanse us from all unrighteousness. ¹⁰ If we say we have not sinned, we make him a liar, and his word is not in us.

Observing the Text

What lie does John warn us about?

_____

_____

_____

What are the benefits of "walking in the light"?

_____

WEEK 4: WALK IN THE LIGHT

_____
_____

How does John describe people who hide or deny their sin?
_____
_____
_____

Interpreting the Text

How is "walking in darkness" different from "walking in the light"?
_____
_____
_____

Do you think John is talking about people who deny they have any sin or those who deny sin in certain areas of their lives?
_____
_____
_____

What is the requirement to be cleansed of unrighteousness?
_____
_____
_____

Teaching

One of the biggest barriers to Christianity for people outside the church is the observation that Christians are hypocrites—we say we believe one way but live a different way. That observation is affirmed when they experience people who claim to be Christians but who are rude, uncaring, and judgmental. Another barrier to Christianity is the misconception outside the church that because someone claims to be a Christian they are, or should be, perfect—never rude, never sinful, and never unkind.

At first pass, you might think John says the same thing: that a true Christian lives a faultless life.

> *"...God is light, and in him is no darkness at all. If we say we have fellowship with him while we walk in darkness, we lie and do not practice the truth."*
>
> —1 John 1:5-6

But read this whole text carefully. John doesn't say that to walk in the light means that we are sinless. Rather, he says that to walk in the light is to bring our sinfulness into the light with us. John has the same problem with some "Christians" that many unchurched people do. That is, some claim to be righteous (meaning they have a right life and relationship with God) when they clearly are not, yet they deny their unrighteousness. To walk in darkness doesn't necessarily mean your life is given over to sin, it simply means that you keep the sin in your life hidden while claiming to follow Jesus. Or, you deny that the sin in your life really is sin, defining sin according to your standards rather than submitting to God's authority.

John uses a harsh word to describe these kind of people: liars. They lie to God, to others, and to themselves. *"If we say we have no sin we deceive ourselves"* (verse 8). This is a scary and dangerous way to live. To deny our sinfulness is to deny our need for Christ. To deny our sinfulness is to believe we have fellowship with God on our own merits. To deny our sinfulness is to live in an unbiblical relationship with God that is not rooted in truth and grace, but is still lost in the basic sin of demanding to rule our lives in God's place. To deny our sinfulness is to call God a liar, claiming that his work on the cross was unnecessary and meaningless.

The antidote to all this is simple: tell the truth. Don't fake it. Hidden sin keeps us in darkness but confessed sin brings forgiveness and cleansing. While hidden sin separates us from God and others, confessed sin unites. The single biggest barrier to anyone's spiritual life and growth is the sin they hold on to and hide; engage in but deny.

You are called by God to walk in the light. There are no fakers in the Kingdom of Heaven. God knows your heart, he knows what you think, and sees your every action. You cannot escape the truth of God. He is God and he is sovereign.

There is a phrase used in AA meetings: "Your secrets will kill you." That is true. Your secrets will keep you in darkness and your secrets are what allow you to deceive yourself. So do the only thing that makes any sense at all for an adopted child of God the Father: tell the truth. Don't hide. The family you have been adopted into is the perfect forum for confessing your sin and struggle. Your honesty in front of others means you are taking your identity as God's adopted child seriously. Have real faith in Jesus. Be bold! Be honest! Bring what is hidden into the light.

Questions for Reflection

Do you ever think of yourself as a hypocrite? If so, when and why?

_____
_____
_____

Do you have behaviors in your life that you accept but God condemns? What truths are you not wanting to hear from his word?

_____
_____

LIVING **INTERDEPENDENTLY**

Do you agree that the single biggest barrier to a person's spiritual growth is the sin they refuse to confess? Why or why not?

Prayer

Ask God to show you any areas in your life where you could rightly be called hypocritical and acknowledge your sin to him honestly.

SCRIPTURE MEMORY

_____, he is faithful and just to forgive us our sins and to _____ from all unrighteousness.

—*1 John 1:9*

LIVING **INTERDEPENDENTLY**

DAY
2

THE CONNECTING POWER OF CONFESSION

Scripture Study

1 JOHN 1:5-10

This is the message we have heard from him and proclaim to you, that God is light, and in him is no darkness at all. ⁶ If we say we have fellowship with him while we walk in darkness, we lie and do not practice the truth. ⁷ But if we walk in the light, as he is in the light, we have fellowship with one another, and the blood of Jesus his Son cleanses us from all sin. ⁸ If we say we have no sin, we deceive ourselves, and the truth is not in us. ⁹ If we confess our sins, he is faithful and just to forgive us our sins and to cleanse us from all unrighteousness. ¹⁰ If we say we have not sinned, we make him a liar, and his word is not in us.

Observing the text

Who do we have fellowship with as we walk in the light?

_____
_____
_____

WEEK 4: WALK IN THE LIGHT

What are we to do with our sins?

_____
_____
_____

List the things that happen when we confess sin.

_____
_____
_____

Interpreting the text

What does confessing sin have to do with "walking in the light"?

_____
_____
_____

Who is impacted when we confess our sins and walk in the light?

_____
_____
_____

What is the relationship between confessing our sin and having God's word in us?

_____
_____
_____

Teaching

> *But if we walk in the light, as he is in the light, we have fellow-*

> ship with one another, and the blood of Jesus his Son cleanses us from all sin. (v. 7)

If we walk in the light, that is, if we tell the truth about our sinfulness and our need for Jesus, we have "fellowship with one another." Fellowship is a significant word in the New Testament. It means "full participation with." "Fellowship" represents the human experience that accurately reflects the intimate and communal relationship of our triune God, Father, Son and Spirit. This fellowship is summed up by Jesus when he prays for his disciples "…that they may be one, even as we are one" (John 17:11).

To "walk in the light" means to trust Jesus as Savior, to seek to submit our lives to his Lordship, and to confess when and how we sin. John makes the remarkable statement that when people follow Jesus together, and tell the truth when they struggle with sin, they can experience not just friendship or spiritual growth, but true *fellowship*.

It all starts with telling the truth about yourself:

- Confession gives everyone else the permission to be truthful about themselves.
- Confession is the antidote for hypocrisy.
- Confession testifies to your real and practical need for Jesus and his gospel in a way everyone can understand.
- Confession allows others to identify with you because they can connect with your weaknesses more deeply than they can with your victories.
- Confession articulates a need for grace that others share but might not be able to express, helping them see themselves rightly.
- Confession brings the truth of God's word into everyday life in a way that others can understand and identify with.
- Confession demonstrates at least the initial step of repentance for others.

- Confession helps transform your group into a place where the gospel of Jesus is at work in real time.

All of these things break down barriers between people, strengthen the common purpose of a group of Christians, and move the group into the spiritual realm where the gospel is essential and active. Fellowship becomes possible when more than one person believes the truth and grace of Jesus enough to repent, and then talk openly and honestly about their life in light of God's word and wisdom.

If we really believe Jesus came in truth and grace, then we believe he hears our confession of sin and that we are forgiven and cleansed. We must learn to be people who joyfully and willingly do the same for each other. When we do, we can walk in the light together.

Questions for Reflection

How do you react to another person's honest confession of sin?

_____
_____
_____

How does confession of sin help a small group grow as disciples?

_____
_____
_____

Do you think it is worth the risk of confessing your sin for the possibility of experiencing fellowship with other believers? If so, do you and will you?

_____
_____
_____

LIVING **INTERDEPENDENTLY**

Prayer

Ask God to transform your group into a place where it is normal and healthy to confess sin.

SCRIPTURE MEMORY

If we confess our sins, he is _____ _____ to forgive us our sins and to cleanse us _____.

—1 John 1:9

LIVING **INTERDEPENDENTLY**

DAY
3

TRUTH AND GRACE

Scripture Study

1 JOHN 1:5-10

This is the message we have heard from him and proclaim to you, that God is light, and in him is no darkness at all. ⁶ If we say we have fellowship with him while we walk in darkness, we lie and do not practice the truth. ⁷ But if we walk in the light, as he is in the light, we have fellowship with one another, and the blood of Jesus his Son cleanses us from all sin. ⁸ If we say we have no sin, we deceive ourselves, and the truth is not in us. ⁹ If we confess our sins, he is faithful and just to forgive us our sins and to cleanse us from all unrighteousness. ¹⁰ If we say we have not sinned, we make him a liar, and his word is not in us.

JOHN 1:12-13

But to all who did receive him, who believed in his name, he gave the right to become children of God, ¹³ who were born, not of blood nor of the will of the flesh nor of the will of man, but of God.

MATTHEW 9:36

When he saw the crowds, he had compassion for them, because they were harassed and helpless, like sheep without a shepherd.

WEEK 4: WALK IN THE LIGHT

Observing the Text

How do these texts describe Jesus's reaction to our sin?

_____
_____
_____

How are we cleansed from the sin we confess?

_____
_____
_____

How many times does 1 John 1:5-10 use the word, *we* or *us*?

_____
_____
_____

Interpreting the Text

What does Matthew mean by the way that he describes the crowds Jesus saw?

_____
_____
_____

How could Jesus have chosen to react to the people in the crowds?

_____
_____
_____

Why does 1 John say Jesus is "just" to forgive our sins? What makes his forgiveness justice and not simply kindness?

_____

LIVING **INTERDEPENDENTLY**

Teaching

Do you ever wonder what Jesus thinks of all the people these days who are devoted to marijuana, who are messing up their marriage, who cheat other people for money, who are committing violent crimes, who produce pornography, etc.? The answer, found in Matthew 9:36, is that he has *compassion* for them.

Jesus looks on the messes that people have made through sinfulness, and his response isn't anger. Jesus isn't vengeful or hateful or disgusted. He sees people who need help. Jesus sees people who have no purpose or direction or benevolent leadership. Jesus sees people harassed by the materialistic values and demands of sin-corrupted culture and the consequences of personal selfishness. Jesus sees people who are vulnerable to being led anywhere; like sheep, they follow into danger because they are helpless to do otherwise. Jesus has *compassion* for them.

The quality of our relationships as a spiritual family who truly love and serve each other is going to depend on how we respond to each other when there is sin. The picture John paints in 1 John 1:5-10 is a picture of the way God's family responds to the truth about each other—truth leads to *fellowship*.

John uses the word *"we"* thirteen times and the word *"us"* another five times in just six verses. A fellowship-producing response to sin comes from recognizing in each other both our family resemblance as habitual sinners *and* the family resemblance we have to our loving and gracious Father. We are being forgiven and being made righteous at the same time. We can respond to the truth about each other in one of two ways. First, we can use the truth as a weapon. We can use the truth to punish or ostracize people, or we can use it as a lever to control them. We can do a tremendous amount of harm to someone who shares the truth about themselves in the form of confessed sin. At the very least, our sinful response to their confessed sin can be the reason they don't risk telling the truth the next time.

But there is a second kind of response. We can do great good through our response to the truth. We can prove that God is our true Father and respond to confessed sin the way Jesus responds: we can demonstrate mercy and compassion. We can try to understand (not excuse) and respond in humility and kindness. We can lift each other up in prayer and celebrate that the gospel is good news for everyone who is harassed and helpless, like sheep without a shepherd. We can celebrate that someone has stepped into the light and encourage them with the truth of God's word. We can admit how we have struggled in similar ways or fallen to our own temptations, and, in so doing, build a community where repentance and redemption is the norm.

John 1:12-13 reminds us that none of us entered God's family by the will of flesh or by the will of man. Not one of us is righteous. Not one of us merit our place in God's family. Not one of us in ourselves are worthy to enter the Kingdom of Heaven. We are family because God chose to make us family. God revealed himself to us and adopted us. Jesus came in truth *and grace*—just as much for you as for the person who sits across from you in group confessing a dark and destructive sin.

Handle the truth with grace! Remember compassion, kindness, humility, meekness, and patience. May we learn to value each other as Jesus values us so that the Father's love for his children is reflected in his children's love for one another.

LIVING **INTERDEPENDENTLY**

Questions for Reflection

What has to happen in us so that we are able to have compassion and mercy on others?

_____
_____
_____

How have you personally seen truth used as a destructive weapon?

_____
_____
_____

Do you contribute to an environment in your group where it is safe and beneficial for people to confess sin? In what way?

_____
_____
_____

Prayer

Ask God to grow your heart of understanding and compassion. Ask him to help you shepherd a person through sin but not excuse the person's sin.

WEEKLY EXERCISE

CELEBRATE CONFESSION

Recall the last time someone confessed sin to you, seeking help or forgiveness (it would be great if this is someone from your small group). Write them a note or email explaining how you identify with sin and temptation and why you are grateful for God's adoption into his family for both of you.

WEEK 4: WALK IN THE LIGHT

Get Ready for Group

Write your memorized Scripture.

_____
_____
_____
_____
_____

What observations and interpretations of Scripture were most meaningful to you?

_____
_____
_____
_____
_____

Summarize your key takeaway(s) for this week.

_____
_____
_____
_____
_____

What will you tell the group about the results of your exercise this week?

_____
_____
_____
_____
_____

LIVING **INTERDEPENDENTLY**

How has this week helped you better understand and apply the Spiritual Growth Grid?

_____
_____
_____
_____
_____

		REPENT & BELIEVE	
WHO GOD IS	WHAT GOD DID	WHO WE ARE	WHAT WE DO
KING	CALLED	CITIZENS	LISTEN & OBEY
FATHER	ADOPTED	FAMILY	LOVE & SERVE
SAVIOR	SENT	MISSIONARIES	GO & MULTIPLY

05

CHANGE BEGINS IN THE HEART

SCRIPTURE MEMORY

Therefore, confess your sins to one another and pray for one another, that you may be healed. The prayer of a righteous person has great power as it is working.

—*James 5:16*

LIVING **INTERDEPENDENTLY**

DAY 1

POINT TO JESUS

Scripture Study

LUKE 6:43-45

"For no good tree bears bad fruit, nor again does a bad tree bear good fruit, ⁴⁴ for each tree is known by its own fruit. For figs are not gathered from thornbushes, nor are grapes picked from a bramble bush. ⁴⁵ The good person out of the good treasure of his heart produces good, and the evil person out of his evil treasure produces evil, for out of the abundance of the heart his mouth speaks.

Observing the Text

How can you identify the type of a tree or bush?
_____
_____
_____

What is the source of a person's words?
_____
_____
_____

WEEK 5: CHANGE BEGINS IN THE HEART

How does Jesus describe our "treasure"?
_____
_____
_____

Interpreting the Text

According to this passage, what produces a person's actions or words?
_____
_____
_____

What is the point of Jesus's metaphor?
_____
_____
_____

Teaching

In Luke 6:43-35 Jesus makes a simple but profound observation: The fruit a plant produces is always proof of the plant's identity. If you aren't sure what kind of plant it is, you just have to wait for its fruit. Once you see the fruit you know with certainty the type of plant. It is also true that, no matter how hard you try, your thorn bush won't yield grapes or figs. It simply cannot because there are no grapes or figs within it. Thorn bushes have different DNA than grape vines.

Jesus applies this simple truth about plants to people. A person, just like a plant, can only produce fruit in keeping with their identity. The determining factor in the fruit produced in a person's life, their fruit-producing DNA if you will, is what treasure rules the person's heart. From evil treasure you

LIVING **INTERDEPENDENTLY**

get evil; from good treasure you get good. When Jesus says "out of the abundance of the heart his mouth speaks," he is saying that, just like a plant, a person can only produce words and actions in keeping with who he is at heart.

Writer Paul Tripp captures Jesus' teaching in a principle he calls the Principle of Inescapable Influence: Whatever rules the heart exercises an inescapable influence over a person's life and behavior. All of this means only one thing, if a person is going to truly change he or she must change from the inside out. The root and center of all personal spiritual change is a person's heart.

In the Bible, the heart is the center of all that shapes a person's identity and character - their desires, thinking, and conscience. When a person's desires, thinking, and conscience shift from selfish, worldly pursuits to God-glorifying ones, Scripture defines this shift with the word repentance. Paul Tripp has a useful definition of repentance: a radical change of heart that leads to a radical change of life and behavior.

Jesus was preparing his hearers in Luke 6 to understand that every meaningful and lasting change a person makes begins with God giving them a new heart.

> *And I will give you a new heart, and a new spirit I will put within you. And I will remove the heart of stone from your flesh and give you a heart of flesh.*
> —Ezekiel 36:26

God replaces sin-corrupted thinking with wisdom; God replaces selfish desires with a longing to serve; God transforms our perspective so we see life differently.

WEEK 5: CHANGE BEGINS IN THE HEART

How do these truths intersect with our interpersonal relationships as God's children? Telling the truth about ourselves by confessing our sin and brokenness is not the end of our gospel transformation. It is only the beginning. We recognize and speak our sins in order to offer them, and the part of our hearts from which they come, to God for his mercy and control.

God's family plays a significant role in this process, not only as we encourage and honor confession of sin but also as we admonish and encourage each other to truly surrender to God's lordship, wisdom, and values. We need to always remember that we do not have the power to change another person's heart. We point each other to Jesus. We encourage each other to trust in his gospel. We celebrate each other when sin is confessed and repentance occurs.

A gospel family does not force a system of behaviors on each other. We know from Jesus' teaching in Luke 6 that hanging grapes on a thorn bush does not transform it into a grapevine, so we don't prioritize outward behavior and appearances. We focus on the heart:

- How can we help each other think the way God thinks?
- How can we make sin as repulsive to ourselves as it is to our Father?
- How can we foster in each other a servant's heart that mirrors our Savior's?
- How can we help each other learn to want the same things God wants?

When we hate sin, desire to serve others, and long to worship God with our words and deeds, we will experience repentance through our changed behavior. The work we do together is to help each other grow in our love for Jesus and joy in his gospel so each of us produce good fruit. God's family works together to see God accomplish this in each of us.

LIVING **INTERDEPENDENTLY**

Questions for Reflection

What would Jesus say about forcing religious rules on others to get them to obey God?

_____
_____
_____

How would you define repentance? What does it look like?

_____
_____
_____

Why is it important to understand that lasting change begins in the heart?

_____
_____
_____

Prayer

Think of another person in your life who is struggling with sin. Pray that God would change their heart and bring them to repentance.

SCRIPTURE MEMORY

Therefore, _____ your sins to one another and _____ for one another, that you may be healed. The prayer of a righteous person has great power as it is _____.

—*James 5:16*

LIVING **INTERDEPENDENTLY**

DAY
2

REPENTANCE IS A VERB

Scripture Study

LUKE 19: 1-10

He entered Jericho and was passing through. ² And behold, there was a man named Zacchaeus. He was a chief tax collector and was rich. ³ And he was seeking to see who Jesus was, but on account of the crowd he could not, because he was small in stature. ⁴ So he ran on ahead and climbed up into a sycamore tree to see him, for he was about to pass that way. ⁵ And when Jesus came to the place, he looked up and said to him, "Zacchaeus, hurry and come down, for I must stay at your house today." ⁶ So he hurried and came down and received him joyfully. ⁷ And when they saw it, they all grumbled, "He has gone in to be the guest of a man who is a sinner." ⁸ And Zacchaeus stood and said to the Lord, "Behold, Lord, the half of my goods I give to the poor. And if I have defrauded anyone of anything, I restore it fourfold." ⁹ And Jesus said to him, "Today salvation has come to this house, since he also is a son of Abraham. ¹⁰ For the Son of Man came to seek and to save the lost."

Observing the text

What is the theme of Luke 19:1-10, and how is it similar to the theme of

WEEK 5: CHANGE BEGINS IN THE HEART

Luke 3:10-14 and Leviticus 6:1-6?

_____
_____
_____

What specific actions are called for in Luke 19:1-10, Luke 3:10-14, and Leviticus 6:1-6?

_____
_____
_____

How does Luke describe Zacchaeus? What does Luke say Zacchaeus was doing?

_____
_____
_____

Interpreting the text

What does Luke's description of Zacchaeus tell us about his character?

_____
_____
_____

Explain Zacchaeus's actions in light of Leviticus 6:1-6.

_____
_____
_____

If Zacchaeus knew the Law (Leviticus 6 specifically), what is significant about his promise to Jesus?

_____
_____

LIVING **INTERDEPENDENTLY**

Teaching

Words are cheap. How many times have you heard someone say one thing but do another? The most important thing to understand about true repentance is that it involves concrete action. Saying "I'm sorry," or "I won't do that again," or "It wasn't my fault," does not constitute repentance.

The story of Jesus and Zacchaeus helps us understand two specific aspects of true repentance. First, repentance begins with grace. Zacchaeus wanted to see Jesus because he had heard about him. He climbed a tree to catch a glimpse from afar because he knew his own heart—that he was sinful and selfish. He had corrupted his life and sold his identity for money. He was an outcast, alone and lost, and he knew it. The news he had heard about Jesus gave him hope that everything he had done to himself and others could be somehow made right. Motivation to change is rooted in a believable vision of a better future. The stories Zacchaeus had heard about Jesus provided him with hope.

Zacchaeus was obviously troubled by his life and the by way he made his money; he was convicted. But, conviction without the possibility of grace does not lead a person to repentance, it leads to hard hearts, excuses, and self-justification. Until Jesus appeared, Zacchaeus betrayed others, defrauded many, and extorted money from people. The hatred and isolation he experienced only served to harden his heart toward the people he cheated. But Jesus responds to Zacchaeus's sin with grace, not condemnation or accusation, but with the good news of the gospel that promises hope for sinners. Jesus responds to Zacchaeus with acceptance. He didn't shun or shame Zacchaeus or excuse his evil, but instead, he gave Zacchaeus the gift of his presence.

WEEK 5: CHANGE BEGINS IN THE HEART

The second thing about true repentance is that it always involves action. Remember Paul Tripp's definition of repentance: "a radical change of heart that leads to a radical change in behavior." Repentance is about what a person does. Zacchaeus proved his repentance by determining he would do different things with his money. He is going to give half of it away and pay restitution to those whom he has cheated. He didn't just say he was sorry and keep the profit. He didn't try to justify his past sinfulness. As Paul tells the Corinthian church:

> *For godly grief produces a repentance that leads to salvation without regret, whereas worldly grief produces death.*
> —2 Corinthians 7:10

Zacchaeus's grief over his sin changed his heart toward money and people, and this change of heart changed what he determined to do with both. He made a bold promise to Jesus, and Jesus believed him, "Today salvation has come to this house."

If we are going to live as God's family, we need to learn about sin and repentance from both Zacchaeus and Jesus. Zacchaeus teaches us that repentance involves a longing for change and a desire for God. That's what Zacchaeus wanted when he climbed the tree. Jesus responds to Zacchaeus with grace and welcome, giving him hope that change was possible. When we have embraced hope in the gospel of Jesus, repentance will always impact what we do, starting from right where we are. The glory of God's grace at work in our heart will produce a radically new way of thinking and living. As a family, we help each other repent when we ask each other about actions and choices, and don't settle for regrets and excuses. We help each other "climb the tree."

LIVING **INTERDEPENDENTLY**

Questions for Reflection

Why is extending grace essential to helping someone repent?

_____
_____
_____

What role did the Good News of the gospel pay in Zacchaeus's repentance?

_____
_____
_____

Do you think repentance really does begin with grace? Explain why or why not.

_____
_____
_____

Prayer

Ask God to show you what actions you need to take to demonstrate repentance of sin. Then go do whatever it is.

SCRIPTURE MEMORY

Therefore, confess your sins to ___ ____ and pray for _____, that you may be healed. The _____ of a righteous person has great power as it is working.

—*James 5:16*

LIVING **INTERDEPENDENTLY**

DAY
3

THE MEAT AND BONES OF REPENTANCE

Scripture Study

LEVITICUS 6:1-6

The Lord spoke to Moses, saying, [2] "If anyone sins and commits a breach of faith against the Lord by deceiving his neighbor in a matter of deposit or security, or through robbery, or if he has oppressed his neighbor [3] or has found something lost and lied about it, swearing falsely—in any of all the things that people do and sin thereby—[4] if he has sinned and has realized his guilt and will restore what he took by robbery or what he got by oppression or the deposit that was committed to him or the lost thing that he found [5] or anything about which he has sworn falsely, he shall restore it in full and shall add a fifth to it, and give it to him to whom it belongs on the day he realizes his guilt. [6] And he shall bring to the priest as his compensation to the Lord a ram without blemish out of the flock, or its equivalent, for a guilt offering.

WEEK 5: CHANGE BEGINS IN THE HEART

Observing the Text

What examples of sin are given in Leviticus 6:1-6?

_____
_____
_____

How is the sinner told to make it right with other people? How should he make it right with the Lord?

_____
_____
_____

What goal does God give in Leviticus 6:1-6 for why he asks the sinner to make it right?

_____
_____
_____

Interpreting the Text

In Leviticus 6:1-6, why do you think God commands the addition of a fifth to what has been taken?

_____
_____
_____

In Leviticus 6:1-6, why does the sinner have to address both the person they injured and God?

_____
_____
_____

What does the Bible's teaching about sin and restoration teach us about repentance?

_____

_____

_____

Teaching

The instructions about restitution in Leviticus 6 (see also Numbers 5 and Exodus 22) were given by God as he established the people of Israel as a nation. For decades they had been ruled by the Egyptians and had no social structure of their own, let alone one that was submitted to God and glorifying to him. It is a good text to examine as we consider what's required for us to live together as God's family. It reveals some essential elements for living in a gospel community in the modern world.

The first thing to notice is that God calls all the examples of offenses against others "sin" and a "breach of faith against the Lord." How different our relationships would be if we really accepted that when we cheat or lie or take advantage of someone—even in small ways—we sin against our Lord! Sin is never trivial before God.

Next, God establishes a practice that we must include in our relationships if we are to have any hope of enjoying true repentance and forgiveness when we sin against each other. The practice is simple: always address the material effects of the offense. According to Leviticus 6, *restitution* is the action that results when repentance really happens in the heart—the physical expression of repentance. In Leviticus 6 we see that restitution involved the offender, the offended, and the priest.

WEEK 5: CHANGE BEGINS IN THE HEART

God is wise, and he knows that when an offense is committed, avoiding or covering over the issue only keeps the peace on the surface. If the offense isn't addressed directly, the wounds and mistrust remain. People stay separated. So, God instituted a formal practice of dealing with the material part of the sin so that the relational part of the sin can be addressed in a healthy way. The purpose of the practice is of the relationship.

Restitution involves a public confession of guilt and public acceptance of personal responsibility for the consequences of the sin. In Leviticus, not only does the offender repay what was taken, but he also adds twenty percent as a penalty and apology. This instruction implies that there must be some agreement of value, and probably a third party would help determine what is appropriate. On the same day the offender makes restitution to the offended, he offers a guilt offering to the Lord because his sin not only injured the person but also broke faith with God. Both are addressed.

What often happens when an offending person is confronted and asked to participate in a process of repentance and restitution is they just leave the church or group. Avoiding people who want to help may seem easier than facing up to the public nature of true repentance, but there is no restoration in denying or running away from the consequences of sin, with people or with God. Separating one's self from the family doesn't bring healing it just causes more pain.

People are sinful and broken. We are prone to selfishness and resentment. But, God is merciful and forgiving. In Christ, we can trust God to love and accept us in our weakness and to welcome our repentance. How glorifying it is to God when an offending person is truly sorry and willingly offers repentance demonstrated by restitution! How glorifying to God when the injured person freely accepts the restitution and forgives the offender! Everyone involved can bring praise to God and bring peace to people. That is what God's family is supposed to do.

LIVING **INTERDEPENDENTLY**

Questions for Reflection

What have you seen most, people leaving a relationship or people going through the process of confessing, repenting, and making restitution?

_____
_____
_____

Why is it such a negative thing when people change churches or groups to avoid the work and cost of reconciling relationships? What can be done to keep people from taking the easy way out?

_____
_____
_____

What happens in the heart of the offender and the offended when there is unwillingness to make restitution or unwillingness to accept it?

_____
_____
_____

Prayer

Ask God to show you if there is anyone to whom you need to offer restitution for something you did.

WEEKLY EXERCISE

PRACTICING REPENTANCE

Write down the practical steps you would take to repent and make restitution for the following sins:

You told a lie to avoid having to go to a party you didn't want to attend.

_____
_____
_____

You accidentally took your friend's Yeti home with you, but you just never gave it back. Now you've had it for months.

_____
_____
_____

You told your boss you were leaving early and would work extra this weekend. But you didn't.

_____
_____
_____

Your neighbor told you that their kid lost a toy that was precious to them. As he told you, you realized your child had it, but you didn't say anything.

_____
_____
_____

You were volunteering at a church event last week, and while you were helping set up you noticed several boxes of packaged cookies in a closet. You were hungry, so you ate a few when no one was looking.

_____
_____
_____

WEEK 5: CHANGE BEGINS IN THE HEART

Get Ready for Group

Write your memorized Scripture.

What observations and interpretations of Scripture were most meaningful to you?

Summarize your key takeaway(s) for this week.

What will you tell the group about the results of your exercise this week?

LIVING **INTERDEPENDENTLY**

How has this week helped you better understand and apply the Spiritual Growth Grid?

_____
_____
_____
_____
_____

	REPENT & BELIEVE		
WHO GOD IS	WHAT GOD DID	WHO WE ARE	WHAT WE DO
KING	CALLED	CITIZENS	LISTEN & OBEY
FATHER	ADOPTED	FAMILY	LOVE & SERVE
SAVIOR	SENT	MISSIONARIES	GO & MULTIPLY

06

PRAY FOR ONE ANOTHER

SCRIPTURE MEMORY

Therefore, confess your sins to one another and pray for one another, that you may be healed. The prayer of a righteous person has great power as it is working

—*James 5:16*

LIVING **INTERDEPENDENTLY**

DAY 1

PRAY FOR EACH OTHER

Scripture Study

JAMES 5:13-20

Is anyone among you suffering? Let him pray. Is anyone cheerful? Let him sing praise. [14] Is anyone among you sick? Let him call for the elders of the church, and let them pray over him, anointing him with oil in the name of the Lord. [15] And the prayer of faith will save the one who is sick, and the Lord will raise him up. And if he has committed sins, he will be forgiven. [16] Therefore, confess your sins to one another and pray for one another, that you may be healed. The prayer of a righteous person has great power as it is working. [17] Elijah was a man with a nature like ours, and he prayed fervently that it might not rain, and for three years and six months it did not rain on the earth. [18] Then he prayed again, and heaven gave rain, and the earth bore its fruit.

[19] My brothers, if anyone among you wanders from the truth and someone brings him back, [20] let him know that whoever brings back a sinner from his wandering will save his soul from death and will cover a multitude of sins.

WEEK 6: PRAY FOR ONE ANOTHER

Observing the Text

In what situations are we commanded to pray? How many times does James mention prayer in this text?

What different things will prayer accomplish?

How is Elijah described?

Interpreting the Text

Why does James call us to pray in these various situations?

Who qualifies as a righteous person whose prayer will have great power? Do you?

LIVING **INTERDEPENDENTLY**

What is significant about James connecting the comment about "bringing back a sinner" to exhortation to pray?

_____

_____

_____

Teaching

James 5:13-20 is one of those texts in the Bible that confuses a lot of people. James seems to oversimplify things. It sounds like he is saying, "You know someone who is suffering? Know anyone who is sick? Just call the elders. They will rub on a little oil, say a prayer, and 'poof' instant healing!" On one hand, it makes us feel kind of guilty if we're not completely convinced God really will heal on demand, so we don't pray like that. On the other hand, experience tells us God very often *doesn't* heal on demand. So, how do we make sense of what James is saying so we can believe and pray like James describes?

James isn't trying to be confusing. Look closely at the text and consider the issue James is actually addressing. He makes specific promises about what God will do as a result of prayer: people will be saved, raised up, and forgiven. It sounds like James is thinking spiritually when he says "that you may be *healed*." In the following part of the text, James applies the example of Elijah's faithful prayer to our involvement in saving a sinner's soul from death and covering his sins. James isn't trying to answer all of our questions about how prayer works. He is teaching us something essential about the spiritual power of prayer as it works among the members of God's family.

We don't like to admit it, but the Bible repeatedly makes this connection: suffering and even physical sickness is often caused by the personal choices we make. They don't necessarily have to be drastic, overtly rebellious choices like drunkenness or adultery. People suffer physically from the anxiety of being poor stewards of their money or their time, from the relational consequences of gossip or selfishness, or from resisting the role God has given them in their families. James is addressing the physical suffering people endure because they have "wandered from the truth." Most of the time, we wander away from the truth in subtle ways. And often, the consequences of our wandering are more readily apparent than their cause.

James teaches us something about prayer that isn't glamorous or all that mysterious. He is teaching us a practical lesson in how to care spiritually for each other, that we must pray with and for each other about our sin. We are often reluctant to believe our prayers for the spiritual struggle of another person will result in dramatic change. But James says, have no doubt! Our prayer can lead to healing, salvation, and life. This commitment to pray requires a willingness to enter each other's worlds and bring truth. We must help each other examine how and where our thinking and behavior remain resistant to God's will and rule. We must be willing to hear and honestly consider what others say about our own sin. Above all, we must realize we are all dependent on God's grace and the power of the Spirit to change hearts. So, we must continually pray.

James is challenging us as a family to care about the pain and suffering we all experience due to sin and to pray fervently for each other. He is challenging us to admit that our choices have consequences. And he is challenging us to pray for each other believing that God forgives our sin, God changes the desires of our hearts, and that spiritual healing brings physical healing. "The prayer of a righteous person has great power as it is working," (James 5:16)

Questions for Reflection

What keeps you from praying fervently for God to heal?

_____
_____
_____

Do you believe we suffer physically because of sin? Have you seen this in your own life?

_____
_____
_____

What do you think would happen if you really did come out and confess all your sins to other people in your group? Would they pray with you and for you?

_____
_____
_____

Prayer

Pray that God will make your group a place where the confession and prayer James commands is a normal part of the community.

SCRIPTURE MEMORY

Therefore, _____ to one another and _____, that you may be healed. The prayer of a _____ has great power as it is working

—*James 5:16*

LIVING **INTERDEPENDENTLY**

DAY
2

THE POWER OF PRAYER

Scripture Study

JAMES 5:13-20

Is anyone among you suffering? Let him pray. Is anyone cheerful? Let him sing praise. [14] Is anyone among you sick? Let him call for the elders of the church, and let them pray over him, anointing him with oil in the name of the Lord. [15] And the prayer of faith will save the one who is sick, and the Lord will raise him up. And if he has committed sins, he will be forgiven. [16] Therefore, confess your sins to one another and pray for one another, that you may be healed. The prayer of a righteous person has great power as it is working. [17] Elijah was a man with a nature like ours, and he prayed fervently that it might not rain, and for three years and six months it did not rain on the earth. [18] Then he prayed again, and heaven gave rain, and the earth bore its fruit.

[19] My brothers, if anyone among you wanders from the truth and someone brings him back, [20] let him know that whoever brings back a sinner from his wandering will save his soul from death and will cover a multitude of sins.

WEEK 6: PRAY FOR ONE ANOTHER

Observing the text

What words and phrases does James use to describe effective prayer?

_____
_____
_____

Interpreting the text

Why does James describe effective prayer as "prayer of faith" and the prayer of a "righteous person"? What did he mean by those descriptions?

_____
_____
_____

Why do you think James uses the example of Elijah? How does what God did in response to Elijah's prayer help us understand how James is calling us to pray?

_____
_____
_____

What kind of power does James say our prayer can have?

_____
_____
_____

Teaching

This text offers us a glimpse into how we can participate in the eternal power of the Father and encourages us to do just that. Listen to what James says: "The prayer of faith will save the one who is sick… if he has committed sins he will be forgiven... whoever brings back a sinner from his wondering will save his soul from death." Those are amazing and far-reaching assertions about the power of prayer. Because of our prayers, God might save a sick person, forgive someone's sins, or save them from death!

There are two keys in the text to help us embrace James's promise with confidence. First, he describes this prayer as the "prayer of faith" and the "prayer of a righteous person." This is not a call to "name it and claim it." We do not control or compel God to act as we wish by the nature of our prayers. A person of faith—a righteous person—is someone who believes whole-heartedly in Jesus and his gospel. A righteous person lives life "in Christ," submitted to the Word of God and seeking to bring glory to God by what they think, say, and do. God's will and their trust in God's sovereignty shape their desires and their prayer. A righteous person loves God so much that he actually wants what God wants. There is great power in the prayer of those who are in tune with God's will and purpose and whose prayers bring that kind of faith and worship to bear on physical and spiritual problems.

James uses Elijah as an example of a person who had the kind of right and faithful relationship with God that he is challenging you to enjoy. James describes Elijah as "a man with a nature like ours." Elijah wasn't Jesus or an angel or some kind of supernatural being. He was just like you and me, and he prayed with inexplicable effect. God heard him and literally modified the weather (1 Kings 17).

We are called and adopted into God's family to provide a caring and concerned community that is devoted to seeing the gospel of Jesus become the motivation for everything we think, say, and do. James concludes this section about the power of prayer by reminding us that just as Elijah's life was completely immersed in God's activity among his people, so your life is to be immersed in God's activity among the people he has providentially gathered in the community of your small group. Just as Elijah's prayer had the power to stop and start the rain, your prayer has the power to restore a sinner who has wandered away back to the family of God. Your prayer has the power to cover over a multitude of sins by leading the wanderer to repentance and faith. Your prayer has the power to help change a wanderer's road from leading to death to the road leading to life in Christ. "The prayer of a righteous person has great power!"

If a group did little else but believe the promise of prayer contained in James 5, and committed themselves to the regular confession of sin and prayer for each other, much would change. God would use them to change each other, their families, their church, and their community.

Mutual confessions and prayers would work to bind together a family who understands and identifies with each other's sin and struggle. Their hearts would be mutually softened, meeting confession with ready forgiveness. They would serve as a continual reminder that our gospel family exists only because the common need for grace in every person has been satisfied in Christ Jesus.

Let us invoke the eternal power, mercy, and grace of God for each other in continual prayer.

Questions for Reflection

What skepticism do you have about the power of prayer as James describes it? Why?

_____
_____
_____

LIVING **INTERDEPENDENTLY**

How would mutual confession and prayer lead to a group of people "living interdependently"?
_____
_____
_____

When have you seen examples of how prayer can lead people from sin to salvation?
_____
_____
_____

Prayer

Ask God to convince you that he hears and responds to your prayers just as much as he heard Elijah's.

SCRIPTURE MEMORY

_____, confess your sins to one another and pray for one another, that _____. The _____ _____ has great power as it is working

—*James 5:16*

LIVING **INTERDEPENDENTLY**

DAY 3

PRAYER BRINGS HEALTH AND UNITY

Scripture Study

MATTHEW 5:43-48

"You have heard that it was said, 'You shall love your neighbor and hate your enemy.' ^{44} But I say to you, Love your enemies and pray for those who persecute you, ^{45} so that you may be sons of your Father who is in heaven. For he makes his sun rise on the evil and on the good, and sends rain on the just and on the unjust. ^{46} For if you love those who love you, what reward do you have? Do not even the tax collectors do the same? ^{47} And if you greet only your brothers, what more are you doing than others? Do not even the Gentiles do the same? ^{48} You therefore must be perfect, as your heavenly Father is perfect.

Observing the Text

What is the key difference between the focus of prayer in this text and James 5:13-20?

_____

_____

_____

How would you summarize what Jesus asks in Matthew 5:43-48?

What are the results of praying for healing (in James 5) and for our enemies (in Matthew 5)? Are these results material or spiritual?

Interpreting the Text

How does Jesus define "love" and "perfection" in Matthew 5:43-48?

What do "tax collectors and Gentiles" do that Jesus tells his followers is not reflective of God's children?

Teaching

In this section of the Sermon on the Mount, Jesus upends the way we naturally respond to people who oppose us or dislike us. He teaches that God doesn't respond to his enemies the way people do. God is gracious to both the good and the bad, sending rain and sun regardless of their morality or beliefs.

LIVING **INTERDEPENDENTLY**

Jesus then points out that even people who know nothing about God love the people who agree with them and love them back. If we love people who love us and hate people who hate us, we are only doing what unbelievers do. As we grow into our identity as God's children, Jesus makes it clear that the way we respond to our enemies is a measure of how much of our Father's character is present in us.

Sometimes when we read passages of Scripture such as this section of the Sermon on the Mount where Jesus calls his followers to a radical new way of life, we gloss over them as being an exaggeration or as not actually relating to us. Or, we think to apply it in only the most extreme situations. In the case of Matthew 5:43-48, we think of "loving our enemies" in extreme circumstances like divorce, abuse, or murder. Jesus's command certainly applies to all these situations, but it also applies to the minor, and even petty, conflicts we experience every day. You cannot exempt yourself from Jesus's command to "love your enemies," if your enemy is just an annoying neighbor or an overbearing boss. You cannot disregard what Jesus says when responding to an inconsiderate driver or the guy who just always seems to disagree with you.

As we grow together as a family, living interdependent lives of service and fellowship, we must apply what Jesus says about enemies to the people we call brothers and sisters in Christ. Consider how Jesus's command might show up in the everyday relational tensions that arise from living in close proximity to other people:

- How can you love the person who raises their children with behaviors you consider inappropriate?
- How do you love the person who takes credit for some good thing you did?
- How do you love the person who eats all the snacks but never brings any?

- How do you love the person who blames everyone else, including you, for their problems but refuses personal responsibility?
- How do you love the person who always insists on interpreting the Bible in a way that excuses or justifies their sinful choices?

In light of what Jesus says, these are the kinds of questions your group will need to answer. How will you respond to the person in your family (church or small group) who opposes, offends, or injures you? What will your heart be toward those who just generally live in ways you disagree with and see as destructive? What will your personal response—and the response of your group as a whole—say about you as "sons of your Father who is in heaven?"

Jesus' call is not to an intellectual or passive agreement with him. He commands us to take specific action in regard to our enemies and those who persecute us. He tells us to pray for them. We are commanded to not only pray about difficult situations or how you feel wounded or persecuted, but also to pray for the person who is causing the pain. Pray for their health, pray for their family, pray for their circumstances, pray for their salvation or spiritual growth, and pray for insight into how you can love and serve them. Pray for them.

Questions for Reflection

What situations come to your mind when Jesus talks about enemies and people who persecute you?

_____
_____
_____

LIVING **INTERDEPENDENTLY**

How would you characterize your typical response to your enemies? Are you a "son of your Father who is heaven" or are you more like a "tax collector"?

_____
_____
_____

Why is it critical for a church or small group to grow in how well they are able to obey Jesus's command in Matthew 5:43-48?

_____
_____
_____

Prayer

Ask God to give you the heart he has for his enemies so that you can be a true "son" of his.

WEEKLY EXERCISE

THOUGHTFUL PRAYER

Part 1. Spend a moment praying by name for every person in your small group. List their name and what you prayed about:

_____
_____
_____
_____
_____
_____
_____
_____
_____
_____
_____
_____
_____
_____
_____

Part 2. Write one area of sin in your life you will ask the group to pray about with and for you.

_____
_____
_____
_____
_____
_____

WEEK 6: PRAY FOR ONE ANOTHER

Get Ready for Group

Write your memorized Scripture.

_____
_____
_____
_____
_____

What observations and interpretations of Scripture were most meaningful to you?

_____
_____
_____
_____
_____

Summarize your key takeaway(s) for this week.

_____
_____
_____
_____
_____

What will you tell the group about the results of your exercise this week?

_____
_____
_____
_____
_____

LIVING **INTERDEPENDENTLY**

How has this week helped you better understand and apply the Spiritual Growth Grid?

_____
_____
_____
_____
_____

	REPENT & BELIEVE		
WHO GOD IS	WHAT GOD DID	WHO WE ARE	WHAT WE DO
KING	CALLED	CITIZENS	LISTEN & OBEY
FATHER	ADOPTED	FAMILY	LOVE & SERVE
SAVIOR	SENT	MISSIONARIES	GO & MULTIPLY

07

INCLUDE EVERYONE

SCRIPTURE MEMORY

You shall not take vengeance or bear a grudge against the sons of your own people, but you shall love your neighbor as yourself: I am the Lord.

—*Leviticus 19:18*

LIVING **INDEPENDENTLY**

DAY
1

EVERYONE IS RESPECTED

Scripture Study

LEVITICUS 19:9-18

"When you reap the harvest of your land, you shall not reap your field right up to its edge, neither shall you gather the gleanings after your harvest. [10] And you shall not strip your vineyard bare, neither shall you gather the fallen grapes of your vineyard. You shall leave them for the poor and for the sojourner: I am the Lord your God.

[11] "You shall not steal; you shall not deal falsely; you shall not lie to one another. [12] You shall not swear by my name falsely, and so profane the name of your God: I am the Lord.

[13] "You shall not oppress your neighbor or rob him. The wages of a hired worker shall not remain with you all night until the morning. [14] You shall not curse the deaf or put a stumbling block before the blind, but you shall fear your God: I am the Lord.

[15] "You shall do no injustice in court. You shall not be partial to the poor or

WEEK 7: INCLUDE EVERYONE

defer to the great, but in righteousness shall you judge your neighbor. 16 You shall not go around as a slanderer among your people, and you shall not stand up against the life of your neighbor: I am the Lord.

17 "You shall not hate your brother in your heart, but you shall reason frankly with your neighbor, lest you incur sin because of him. 18 You shall not take vengeance or bear a grudge against the sons of your own people, but you shall love your neighbor as yourself: I am the Lord.

Observing the Text

What are some specific similarities between the text we've been studying from James and this one?

_____
_____
_____

What kinds of people (socially, economically, physically) are mentioned in these texts?

_____
_____
_____

What is the "royal law"?

_____
_____
_____

Interpreting the Text

How does God think differently than we tend to think about rich people and poor people?

_____
_____

LIVING **INTERDEPENDENTLY**

How would you summarize Leviticus 19:9-18 in one sentence?
_____
_____
_____

How can we incur sin because of a neighbor we fail to "reason frankly" with?
_____
_____
_____

Teaching

Leviticus 19:9-18 teaches us about how we are to glorify God in the way we treat other people. The text addresses five general areas where we can either dishonor God or rightly reflect his character: economic resources, truth, power and authority, social institutions, and another person's sin. Look closely at each part of this text.

God says that we are to be intentional about setting aside some of our resources for the benefit of people who are needy; we should plan to do so. The instruction is to have resources both available and accessible to those who need them. God sees the resources that he has graciously given you as part of his provision for other people. The command isn't onerous—not half or a third of your resources—but simply to consider others when you "gather" and intentionally leave some for those who are in need. The command doesn't quantify how much because it is directed at how we think about what we have. God wants us to see our "crops" through the lens of his material grace to us and then for us to realize that we play a part in his material grace toward others.

WEEK 7: INCLUDE EVERYONE

The next thing God says is don't steal, lie, or deal falsely with others. A fundamental aspect of God's holiness is that there is absolutely nothing false, hidden, or deceitful in him. He is completely truthful and transparent in his dealings. Therefore, any form of impure motive or manipulation "profanes his name" because it is a direct assault on his character, especially when we seek to take advantage of others by making ourselves appear to be something we are not or when we misrepresent information to get what we want. Our interactions with each other are to reflect the purity of his interactions with us.

God holds all authority and power, yet Jesus set aside his authority to come and die on a cross for our benefit, using his power to defeat death for us. People who hold authority over others have a special responsibility to use that authority to serve and benefit the people they lead. Consider what Jesus taught about authority:

> *But Jesus called them to him and said, "You know that the rulers of the Gentiles lord it over them, and their great ones exercise authority over them. It shall not be so among you. But whoever would be great among you must be your servant, and whoever would be first among you must be your slave, even as the Son of Man came not to be served but to serve, and to give his life as a ransom for many."*
>
> —Matthew 20:25-28

Authority comes to us in many forms. As parents, supervisors, pastors, or people who are physically healthy, have material resources, etc. Leviticus 19:14 says using that authority to oppress, abuse, or take advantage of others is to not fear God. To misuse authority is to reject God's authority and pervert the blessings he has given you to make yourself more important than others.

LIVING **INTERDEPENDENTLY**

The command to "not stand up against the life of your neighbor" is a prohibition against leveraging any social system to gain personally at the expense of another person. This passage makes it clear that there should never be an instance where a follower of Jesus uses any social institution to gain advantage over someone else. The text includes both formal institutions such as the courts, and informal institutions, such as social networks where slander can be as damaging as an unjust legal judgment. A person who leverages a social institution to gain at the expense of another person sets himself in opposition to God, who humbly and graciously has given everything to bless and provide for the people who are being taken advantage of.

Finally, God says to not leverage another person's sin against them but instead be as forgiving of them as you are of yourself. The instruction is that we address sin directly, frankly, and openly, attempting to resolve it together. We don't use another person's sin to beat them down or justify our mistreatment of them. We don't carry self-righteous bitterness in our hearts against them because they sinned in some way we think we never would. To "hate our neighbor in our heart," is to have a predetermined dislike and disrespect for them. But that is the opposite of how our identity as God's children is to reflect God's character of grace and forgiveness and forbearance with all people.

We learn to live as God's family through growing in the areas God addresses through the law he gave to Israel: generosity, honesty, service, respect, and humility. We bring God glory when these become the defining characteristics of our relationships.

WEEK 7: INCLUDE EVERYONE

Questions for Reflection

How does the way you think about and treat other people reveal how deeply you have accepted your identity as one of God's adopted children?

_____
_____
_____

What area discussed in the devotional do you struggle with most?

_____
_____
_____

What can the people in a small group do to create the kind of community where these sinful attitudes are addressed and eliminated?

_____
_____
_____

Prayer

Ask God to make you more like him by softening your heart toward all people. Pray that he would reveal any ways that you are dishonoring him in how you are treating his children.

SCRIPTURE MEMORY

You _____ take vengeance or bear a grudge against the sons of your own people, but you shall ____ your neighbor as _____: I am the Lord.

—*Leviticus 19:18*

LIVING **INTERDEPENDENTLY**

DAY 2

LOVE AND RESPECT ON PURPOSE

Scripture Study

JAMES 2:1-8

My brothers, show no partiality as you hold the faith in our Lord Jesus Christ, the Lord of glory. [2] For if a man wearing a gold ring and fine clothing comes into your assembly, and a poor man in shabby clothing also comes in, [3] and if you pay attention to the one who wears the fine clothing and say, "You sit here in a good place," while you say to the poor man, "You stand over there," or, "Sit down at my feet," [4] have you not then made distinctions among yourselves and become judges with evil thoughts? [5] Listen, my beloved brothers, has not God chosen those who are poor in the world to be rich in faith and heirs of the kingdom, which he has promised to those who love him? [6] But you have dishonored the poor man. Are not the rich the ones who oppress you, and the ones who drag you into court? [7] Are they not the ones who blaspheme the honorable name by which you were called?

[8] If you really fulfill the royal law according to the Scripture, "You shall love your neighbor as yourself," you are doing well.

WEEK 7: INCLUDE EVERYONE

LEVITICUS 19:9-18

"When you reap the harvest of your land, you shall not reap your field right up to its edge, neither shall you gather the gleanings after your harvest. [10] And you shall not strip your vineyard bare, neither shall you gather the fallen grapes of your vineyard. You shall leave them for the poor and for the sojourner: I am the Lord your God.

[11] *"You shall not steal; you shall not deal falsely; you shall not lie to one another.* [12] *You shall not swear by my name falsely, and so profane the name of your God: I am the Lord.*

[13] *"You shall not oppress your neighbor or rob him. The wages of a hired worker shall not remain with you all night until the morning.* [14] *You shall not curse the deaf or put a stumbling block before the blind, but you shall fear your God: I am the Lord.*

[15] *"You shall do no injustice in court. You shall not be partial to the poor or defer to the great, but in righteousness shall you judge your neighbor.* 16 *You shall not go around as a slanderer among your people, and you shall not stand up against the life of your neighbor: I am the Lord.*

[17] *"You shall not hate your brother in your heart, but you shall reason frankly with your neighbor, lest you incur sin because of him.* [18] *You shall not take vengeance or bear a grudge against the sons of your own people, but you shall love your neighbor as yourself: I am the Lord.*

Observing the text

List the things we are commanded not to do in the Leviticus text.

_____
_____
_____

LIVING **INTERDEPENDENTLY**

How many times does God say "I am the Lord" in these verses? Where is it repeated?

_____
_____
_____

Interpreting the text

Why do you think the emphasis in this text is on the "shall nots"?

_____
_____
_____

Each paragraph in the text addresses a different way we seek personal gain over our "neighbor". What are they?

_____
_____
_____

What do we seek to gain personally by failing to "reason frankly" with a sinful person?

_____
_____
_____

Teaching

These two texts both examine how we should interact with a vast range of people: rich, poor, your "neighbor," your employee (worker), the physically impaired, and your "brother." The list isn't intended to be exhaustive but rather to teach us as God's family to think carefully about other people and how we relate to them. We are to treat everyone with the same favor and deference we have for ourselves, "you shall love your neighbor as yourself."

These texts address several attitudes and behaviors that inhibit, even prevent, followers of Jesus from growing into the unified community God intends to create through his gospel of grace.

- We tend to show favor to wealthy people: we make favorable assumptions about their character, and often we are hoping to gain favor with them and profit in some way.
- We tend to show disrespect for poor people: we make unfavorable assumptions about their character and don't believe their favor can benefit us.
- We tend to see our resources as ours and that we are earning and deserving what we get. As a result, we don't leave margin in our resources to share with those in need.
- We lie to one another to manage our image, cover our mistakes, hide our laziness, or gain advantage. We minimize the damage to others so we can consider our sin trivial.
- We tend to think people who work for us are not equal with us, so in one way or another we withhold from them what they have rightfully earned. We delay or don't pay because it benefits us to keep the resources longer.
- We go through life mostly unaware and often indifferent to the presence of physically impaired people, and we use our health to take advantage of people who are not as strong or capable as we are.

The key to understanding this whole text is in the reason God gives for his commands, "I am the Lord." Obey me, God says, because I have sovereign authority, period. Our obedience must be motivated by a desire to reflect his character. We are to treat each other with the grace, respect, humility,

LIVING **INTERDEPENDENTLY**

and favor that he has given us. Children, do as your Father does!

One of the amazing gifts God gives to his church is the rich diversity found among the people he calls into his family. We are different from each other by gender, race, resources, intellect, physical abilities, geographical influences, personal experience, and so on. Part of growing together as a family is learning to harness the power of that diversity for the sake of the gospel message we are to carry. But we also must understand that the more we learn to truly love and serve each other in the context of all this diversity, the more we reflect the nature of our Father who calls us together and commissions us to love and serve each other.

As you seek to grow together as a group, it is essential that you hear and embrace the message of these passages personally. Root out the subtle ways you think about other people that enable you to feel separate or superior. Learn to give others what you have that they lack, and learn to receive from others what they have that you lack. "Love your neighbor as yourself. I am the Lord."

Questions for Reflection
How does the way you think about and treat other people reveal how deeply you have accepted your identity as one of God's adopted children?

_____

_____

_____

What area discussed in the devotional do you struggle with most?

_____

_____

_____

WEEK 7: INCLUDE EVERYONE

What can the people in a small group do to create the kind of community where these sinful attitudes are addressed and eliminated?

_____
_____
_____

Prayer

Ask God to make you more like him by softening your heart toward all people. Pray that he would reveal any ways that you are dishonoring him in how you are treating his children.

SCRIPTURE MEMORY

You shall not take _____ or bear a _____ against the sons of your own people, but _____ love your neighbor as yourself: I am the Lord.

—*Leviticus 19:18*

LIVING **INTERDEPENDENTLY**

DAY
3

EVERYONE, INCLUDING YOU

Scripture Study

ROMANS 12:1-8

I appeal to you therefore, brothers, by the mercies of God, to present your bodies as a living sacrifice, holy and acceptable to God, which is your spiritual worship. ² Do not be conformed to this world, but be transformed by the renewal of your mind, that by testing you may discern what is the will of God, what is good and acceptable and perfect.

³ For by the grace given to me I say to everyone among you not to think of himself more highly than he ought to think, but to think with sober judgment, each according to the measure of faith that God has assigned. ⁴ For as in one body we have many members, and the members do not all have the same function, ⁵ so we, though many, are one body in Christ, and individually members one of another. ⁶ Having gifts that differ according to the grace given to us, let us use them: if prophecy, in proportion to our faith; ⁷ if service, in our serving; the one who teaches, in his teaching; ⁸ the one who exhorts, in his exhortation; the one who contributes, in generosity; the one who leads, with zeal; the one who does acts of mercy, with cheerfulness.

WEEK 7: INCLUDE EVERYONE

Observing the Text

What do these verses teach you about how you are to think of yourself?

_____
_____
_____

What does Romans 12 say about what we are to do with our bodies?

_____
_____
_____

What specific gifts are mentioned in Romans 12, and how are we to exercise them?

_____
_____
_____

Interpreting the Text

How do "spiritual sacrifice", "worship", and using your gifts work together?

_____
_____
_____

What is required if you are going to think of yourself with sober judgment: attitude, resources, etc.?

_____
_____
_____

LIVING **INTERDEPENDENTLY**

Why is it significant that Paul added a description to emphasize the way each gift is to be exercised?

_____

_____

_____

Teaching

The Bible is clear that as followers of Jesus we are to think and live differently than people in the world ("world" is a summary term in the Bible for people who reject Jesus as Lord and Savior). As Paul sets up his exhortation to use our spiritual gifts for the benefit of the body of Christ he illustrates that a fundamental difference between God's children and the world is found in the way we think about ourselves.

In the world it is "every man for himself," "if it is going to happen it is up to you," and "look out for number one." But Paul says that in God's family we don't see ourselves as the ultimate purpose and objective of our efforts. Instead, we see ourselves as living sacrifices; we see ourselves in light of our desperate need for God's grace and the help of his body, the church; we see ourselves as instruments for God to use in the service of other members in his body. And, we understand that God has given us roles and responsibilities and the abilities to carry them out for the benefit of the whole body of Christ.

One of the most harmful, gospel-limiting behaviors in the church is when we hold on to the sinful belief that our faith is ours alone, to be experienced between "me and God." The Scripture knows of no such thing as an autonomous follower of Jesus. At every turn God calls us to community, to family, and to interdependence. We are described as a body (Romans 12),

WEEK 7: INCLUDE EVERYONE

God's people, the stones that together build a spiritual house (1 Peter 2), and sons of God (Galatians 4)—metaphors that reflect our participation in each other's lives. If we are going to be the people Paul challenges us to be, we must identify what needs to be added to or removed from our lives in order to be "living sacrifices." And, we must do this work knowing that much of it has to do with repenting of our physical and spiritual autonomy as we learn to think and live as part of a body.

Look at the first two verses of Romans 12 again. It is apparent that knowing God's will is not some mysterious ability reserved for the spiritually elite. Instead, when God transforms our minds and renews them away from self-focus and self-centeredness, we begin to discern that his will for us is that we would invest the unique qualities he has given each of us into living interdependently with our brothers and sisters in Christ.

Questions for Reflection

What does it mean to live interdependently?

_____
_____
_____

What do you think of when you think of being a "living sacrifice"? What has to be sacrificed?

_____
_____
_____

What is involved in thinking soberly about yourself when it comes to learning how to live interdependently with others who are members of the body of Christ?

_____
_____

LIVING **INTERDEPENDENTLY**

How willing are you to learn to play your specific part in the body of Christ?
___
___
___

Prayer

Pray that God would show you where you insist on living independently, both for personal pursuits and/or because you don't want to be involved with other messy people.

WEEKLY EXERCISE

BECOMING A BIBLICAL COMMUNITY

Write a paragraph explaining how the commands given in Leviticus 19:9-18 and Romans 12:1-8 work together to describe an interdependent community of God's people. What important things are occurring in the community? Identify two key areas where you can grow in making your group more like what these texts describe.

WEEK 7: INCLUDE EVERYONE

Get Ready for Group

Write your memorized Scripture.

_____
_____
_____
_____
_____

What observations and interpretations of Scripture were most meaningful to you?

_____
_____
_____
_____
_____

Summarize your key takeaway(s) for this week.

_____
_____
_____
_____
_____

What will you tell the group about the results of your exercise this week?

_____
_____
_____
_____
_____

LIVING **INTERDEPENDENTLY**

How has this week helped you better understand and apply the Spiritual Growth Grid?

_____
_____
_____
_____
_____

REPENT & BELIEVE

WHO GOD IS	WHAT GOD DID	WHO WE ARE	WHAT WE DO
KING	CALLED	CITIZENS	LISTEN & OBEY
FATHER	ADOPTED	FAMILY	LOVE & SERVE
SAVIOR	SENT	MISSIONARIES	GO & MULTIPLY

08

BE CONSIDERATE

SCRIPTURE MEMORY

You shall not take vengeance or bear a grudge against the sons of your own people, but you shall love your neighbor as yourself: I am the Lord.

—*Leviticus 19:18*

LIVING **INTERDEPENDENTLY**

DAY
1

EVERYONE IS RESPECTED

Scripture Study

COLOSSIANS 2:6-23

Therefore, as you received Christ Jesus the Lord, so walk in him, ⁷ rooted and built up in him and established in the faith, just as you were taught, abounding in thanksgiving.

⁸ See to it that no one takes you captive by philosophy and empty deceit, according to human tradition, according to the elemental spirits of the world, and not according to Christ. ⁹ For in him the whole fullness of deity dwells bodily, ¹⁰ and you have been filled in him, who is the head of all rule and authority. ¹¹ In him also you were circumcised with a circumcision made without hands, by putting off the body of the flesh, by the circumcision of Christ, ¹² having been buried with him in baptism, in which you were also raised with him through faith in the powerful working of God, who raised him from the dead. ¹³ And you, who were dead in your trespasses and the uncircumcision of your flesh, God made alive together with him, having forgiven us all our trespasses, ¹⁴ by canceling the record of debt that stood against us with its legal demands. This he set aside, nailing it to the cross.

WEEK 8: BE CONSIDERATE

¹⁵ He disarmed the rulers and authorities and put them to open shame, by triumphing over them in him.

¹⁶ Therefore let no one pass judgment on you in questions of food and drink, or with regard to a festival or a new moon or a Sabbath. ¹⁷ These are a shadow of the things to come, but the substance belongs to Christ. ¹⁸ Let no one disqualify you, insisting on asceticism and worship of angels, going on in detail about visions, puffed up without reason by his sensuous mind, ¹⁹ and not holding fast to the Head, from whom the whole body, nourished and knit together through its joints and ligaments, grows with a growth that is from God.

²⁰ If with Christ you died to the elemental spirits of the world, why, as if you were still alive in the world, do you submit to regulations—²¹ "Do not handle, Do not taste, Do not touch" ²² (referring to things that all perish as they are used)—according to human precepts and teachings? ²³ These have indeed an appearance of wisdom in promoting self-made religion and asceticism and severity to the body, but they are of no value in stopping the indulgence of the flesh.

Observing the Text

In verses 8-15, circle the phrase "in him" or "with him." Summarize the point of those verses in one sentence.

_____
_____
_____

What regulations, rules, or observances are mentioned in verses 16-23? Summarize the point of those verses in one sentence.

_____
_____
_____

LIVING **INTERDEPENDENTLY**

What specific things does this text teach that Jesus has done for us?

_____

_____

_____

Interpreting the Text

What does Paul mean by the phrase "in him"?

_____

_____

_____

Note where Paul says "let no one…" What are those people trying to do or teach?

_____

_____

_____

What does Paul say about the value of rules and regulations?

_____

_____

_____

Teaching

One of the most difficult things for followers of Jesus to do to is discern the presence of sin from things that seem distasteful or unwise but are actually spiritually neutral.

We all bring preferences, biases, and religious traditions with us into our relationships. Many times we unconsciously make judgments about another person's faith based on how we perceive what they say or do through the filter of our preferred traditions and practices. When we do, we inhibit our ability to unite as a family of God's children because we have varying opinions about tattoos, music, raising children, hobbies, or church services. We come from widely varying religious backgrounds and we often struggle with being suspicious or even opposed to people who don't share our traditions and practices.

This isn't a new challenge. The Christians in Colossae were surrounded by people who held very diverse beliefs about God and how God should be worshipped. There were those who insisted on keeping the Law of Moses and following all the traditions of the Jewish Pharisees. There were pagan, mystic influences that insisted on harsh treatment of the body as a way to draw near God. No doubt there was much disagreement and division among the church as to what was and wasn't proper behavior for followers of Jesus. Observe what Paul wrote to them: You received *Christ*, walk *in him* (v.6). Be rooted *in him* (v.7). God has put his fullness *in him* and you have been filled *in him* (v.9). You were buried *with him* in baptism and raised *with him* (v.12). God made you alive *with him* (v.13). Paul firmly establishes their identity in Christ. If we have received Christ, this identity is ours as well. We are who we are only because we are in Christ.

God forgave us and cancelled our sin debt in Christ. God disarmed the rulers and authorities in Christ. Because of this, Paul proclaims, no one can disqualify you because you don't practice their religious law or custom. No one's claim of mystical power or spirituality can bind you to their practices or cause you to feel spiritually inferior. Religious practices, claims, restrictions, and regulations have meaning and purpose only when they are submitted to, and focused on Christ. We are adopted by God into his family in Christ, and that identity supersedes any human-derived religious demands.

LIVING **INTERDEPENDENTLY**

There are too many examples of people who perform all kinds of religious practices and follow all kinds of religious regulations but do utterly evil and sinful things. Don't be led down a fruitless path. Endeavor to be in Christ—love him, seek him, follow him, and grow to become like him!

We will remove barriers to trust and community when we devote ourselves to working to grow together in Christ. Every practice, belief, and tradition must be considered in light of the gospel of Jesus. Something has value and power if, as Paul says, it "has its substance in Christ." When we learn to consider our differences in appearance and behavior in light of Christ, we can learn to celebrate and appreciate those differences and avoid division over things that have no significance for those who are in Christ.

Questions for Reflection

What choices or actions cause you to question other people's faith or salvation? How do you go about determining if your concerns are valid?

_____
_____
_____

Think about the people in your group. What religious backgrounds do they come from, and how does that impact the dynamics of your time together?

_____
_____
_____

How can Colossians 2:6-23 help a group of Christians grow in living interdependently?

_____
_____
_____

WEEK 8: BE CONSIDERATE

Prayer

Ask God to show you the preferences and traditions that you have allowed to separate you from other people in your group.

SCRIPTURE MEMORY

You shall not take vengeance or ____ a grudge against the ____ of your own people, but you shall love your neighbor as yourself: _____.

—Leviticus 19:18

LIVING **INTERDEPENDENTLY**

DAY
2

FOR THEIR SAKE

Scripture Study

1 CORINTHIANS 10:23-33

"All things are lawful," but not all things are helpful. "All things are lawful," but not all things build up. ²⁴ Let no one seek his own good, but the good of his neighbor. ²⁵ Eat whatever is sold in the meat market without raising any question on the ground of conscience. ²⁶ For "the earth is the Lord's, and the fullness thereof." ²⁷ If one of the unbelievers invites you to dinner and you are disposed to go, eat whatever is set before you without raising any question on the ground of conscience. ²⁸ But if someone says to you, "This has been offered in sacrifice," then do not eat it, for the sake of the one who informed you, and for the sake of conscience—²⁹ I do not mean your conscience, but his. For why should my liberty be determined by someone else's conscience? ³⁰ If I partake with thankfulness, why am I denounced because of that for which I give thanks?

³¹ So, whether you eat or drink, or whatever you do, do all to the glory of God. ³² Give no offense to Jews or to Greeks or to the church of God, ³³ just as I try to please everyone in everything I do, not seeking my own advantage, but that of many, that they may be saved.

WEEK 8: BE CONSIDERATE

Observing the text

What issue of conscience is Paul addressing in 1 Corinthians 10:23-33?
___
___
___

Whose good are we to seek when making decisions of conscience?
___
___
___

What does Paul say his motivation is for how he chooses when it comes to issues of conscience?
___
___
___

Interpreting the text

How can something be lawful but not helpful?
___
___
___

Explain Paul's argument for partaking freely or refraining.
___
___
___

What is required of us if we are going to incorporate Paul's wisdom into our lives?
___

LIVING **INTERDEPENDENTLY**

Teaching

In the previous devotional, we looked at Colossians 2 and considered Paul's exhortation to resist being trapped by religious traditions or human doctrines. Instead, we believe and rest in the truth that we have salvation and a right relationship with God in Christ. However, that obviously doesn't mean we go about doing whatever we want, however we want. Paul isn't making a case that because we have grace in Christ we are free to be sinful. Here is a reminder about that from Romans 6:

> *What shall we say then? Are we to continue in sin that grace may abound? By no means! How can we who died to sin still live in it? Do you not know that all of us who have been baptized into Christ Jesus were baptized into his death?*
>
> —Romans 6:1-3

There are ways of thinking and behaving that Scripture reveals as sin. Those things that betray Christ as Lord, disregard the character of God, and rebel against God's sovereign authority are not to be part of the lives of those who God has adopted into his family. We reject sin not because some rules were legislated to us, but because in Christ we love God and desire to obey and glorify him.

Yet, there are times when believers choose not to engage in behaviors even though the behavior is not sinful or scripturally prohibited. "All things are lawful, but not all things are helpful. *"All things are lawful, but not all things build up"* (v.23). As a follower of Jesus, there is an overriding question that helps clarify these choices: will my behavior be *helpful*; will it *build* up others? Think about what Paul says as he concludes this text: "I try to please everyone in everything I do, not seeking my own advantage, but that of many, that they may be saved" (v.33).

WEEK 8: BE CONSIDERATE

The issue among Christians in Corinth was tension over whether it was appropriate for a follower of Jesus to eat meat that had been offered as a sacrifice in the worship of a pagan deity. It's understandable that believers struggled with eating that kind of meat. Paul doesn't try to answer the question or pronounce a rule to follow. He addresses the heart of the person making the choice to eat or not to eat.

As followers of Jesus and members of God's family, we should primarily be concerned about how our behavior will affect the spiritual condition of the people who are exposed to it. We should choose not to exercise our freedom in Christ in a given situation if we know that it will cause division or discord with family members who don't feel the same freedoms as we do. Paul emphasizes this throughout the text. He says we should seek to build up; seek the good of our neighbors; consider the sake of another's conscience; seek the advantage of many, that they may be saved.

This is a challenging but God-glorifying way of honoring the freedom we have in Christ. We are not to selfishly assert our rights; doing so would betray the character of Jesus in us. We are to be considerate of other people for the sake of their salvation and spiritual growth.

The truth and wisdom of this text shows up in many practical ways. It includes the clothes we wear, alcohol consumption, social activities, language, and many other decisions we make. If a culturally, ethnically, and traditionally diverse group of people are going to experience living interdependently in Christ, each must learn to submit to the mutual advantage of the other people in the group. We have to care more about each other's spiritual growth than we do about our freedom to engage in any particular behavior. God's family must demonstrate the humility of Jesus toward each other as we help each other grow up in Christ.

LIVING **INTERDEPENDENTLY**

Questions for Reflection

When have you experienced conflict between people who are followers of Jesus because of someone exercising their "freedom"?

_____
_____
_____

What specific issues or behaviors do people in your group differ on?

_____
_____
_____

Why do you think Paul doesn't just give the Corinthians a rule to follow? Why does he teach them about the way he chooses in such a situation?

_____
_____
_____

Prayer

Pray that God would grow a heart of humility in you and in each person in your group.

SCRIPTURE MEMORY

You _____ or bear a grudge against the sons of your own people, but you _____ _____ as yourself: I am the Lord.

—*Leviticus 19:18*

LIVING **INTERDEPENDENTLY**

DAY
3

PAY ATTENTION TO ONE ANOTHER

Scripture Study

EPHESIANS 4:25-32

Therefore, having put away falsehood, let each one of you speak the truth with his neighbor, for we are members one of another. 26 Be angry and do not sin; do not let the sun go down on your anger, 27 and give no opportunity to the devil. 28 Let the thief no longer steal, but rather let him labor, doing honest work with his own hands, so that he may have something to share with anyone in need. 29 Let no corrupting talk come out of your mouths, but only such as is good for building up, as fits the occasion, that it may give grace to those who hear. 30 And do not grieve the Holy Spirit of God, by whom you were sealed for the day of redemption. 31 Let all bitterness and wrath and anger and clamor and slander be put away from you, along with all malice. 32 Be kind to one another, tenderhearted, forgiving one another, as God in Christ forgave you.

WEEK 8: BE CONSIDERATE

Observing the Text

What specific commands are included in Ephesians 4:25-32?

_____
_____
_____

What negative behaviors are described in Ephesians 4:25-32?

_____
_____
_____

What criteria and purpose does Paul give in Ephesians 4:25-32 for what we choose do and how we choose to speak?

_____
_____
_____

Interpreting the Text

What is the central theme and instruction in this text?

_____
_____
_____

What is required of you if you are going to speak in a way that gives grace to those who hear?

_____
_____
_____

LIVING **INTERDEPENDENTLY**

What does Paul mean by the phrase "we are members of one another? (Ephesians 4:25)

_____

_____

_____

Teaching

If you look back on our study of Colossians 3, you will notice there is a lot in common between that text and Ephesians 4. Both address several things that are relevant to our understanding of how a community of people who live interdependently are *considerate of one another*: don't lie, deal with anger in a healthy way, share, be tenderhearted, don't slander or be malicious.

There are two things in the text from Ephesians that we need to explore further. They are found in what Paul says about the way we work and about the way we speak. First, notice the reason behind the command not to steal but instead to labor. More than just pointing out that to steal is sin, Paul writes:

> ...*rather let him labor, doing honest work with his own hands, so that he may have something to share with anyone in need.* (4:28)

We are given a radical new motivation for going to work and earning money and resources—so that we can share them. How much different would your working life be if you went every day so that you would have something to share with those in need? How much differently would you think about the way you work if you believed God provided your job and income to you because you are part of his provision for people who are in need? Embracing this truth will shift our attitude toward work and how we spend the wages we earn.

Paul also addresses our consideration of one another by addressing the way we speak, clarifying the purpose of our speaking.

> *Let no corrupting talk come out of your mouths, but only such as is good for building up, as fits the occasion, that it may give grace to those who hear. (4:29)*

Just as we are to be intentionally considerate of others in the way we work, we are to be intentionally considerate of others when it comes to what we say. We must say only what is "good for building up." The purpose of our words should be to give grace, encourage, inspire, sustain, and edify - never to corrupt or disparage. And, as Paul instructs, our words should "fit the occasion." That means before we speak we must look around at who is present, consider the situation, spiritual maturity, and relational dynamics *before* we start sending words to our tongue. As we studied in 1 Corinthians 10 and Colossians 4, we need to learn to do everything we do with the spiritual welfare of the people around us as a primary concern.

To live interdependently as God's adopted children, we each must learn to be intentional about keeping margins of time and material resources for contributing to the needs of others, remembering that God instructs us to work for that specific purpose. And we need to pay attention to what we say, how we say it, and who will hear what we say, knowing we are commanded to purposefully speak in ways that build others up and communicate the grace of the gospel. There are few better places to practice and grow in these disciplines and purposes than in the relationships God has provided through small group. The kind of interdependence that reflects God's glory and binds his children is rooted in this kind of humble deference to, and consideration of others.

LIVING **INTERDEPENDENTLY**

Questions for Reflection

Do you think about God's purpose for your work being that you have enough to share with others? What would you do differently if you viewed your job this way?

_____
_____
_____

How aware are you of the people who are about to hear what you say? Do you think ahead in order to speak in a way that is considerate and grace giving?

_____
_____
_____

How would real growth in obedience to God regarding your work and words impact the people in your small group?

_____
_____
_____

Prayer

Pray that God would remind you to speak with caring awareness of others and make your words gracious.

WEEKLY EXERCISE

THE WORK OF CONSIDERATION

Answer the following questions about the last time you were involved in a conversation with three or more people.

List the names and gender of the people who heard you speak:
_____
_____
_____
_____
_____

Were they married, parents, divorced, working, students? Describe each one:
_____
_____
_____
_____
_____

Were they followers of Jesus or unchurched? Answer for each one:
_____
_____
_____
_____
_____

Were they married, parents, divorced, working, students? Describe each one:
_____
_____
_____
_____

WEEK 8: BE CONSIDERATE

Grade yourself for how your words affected each individual present:

Could have been corrupting? _____
Definitely were corrupting? _____
Were Edifying and encouraging? _____
Gave grace to each one? _____

Grade yourself for how your words affected each individual present:
A   B   C   D   E   F

LIVING **INTERDEPENDENTLY**

Get Ready for Group

Write your memorized Scripture.

_____
_____
_____
_____
_____

What observations and interpretations of Scripture were most meaningful to you?

_____
_____
_____
_____
_____

Summarize your key takeaway(s) for this week.

_____
_____
_____
_____
_____

What will you tell the group about the results of your exercise this week?

_____
_____
_____
_____
_____

How has this week helped you better understand and apply the Spiritual Growth Grid?

_____
_____
_____
_____
_____

	REPENT & BELIEVE		
WHO GOD IS	WHAT GOD DID	WHO WE ARE	WHAT WE DO
KING	CALLED	CITIZENS	LISTEN & OBEY
FATHER	ADOPTED	FAMILY	LOVE & SERVE
SAVIOR	SENT	MISSIONARIES	GO & MULTIPLY

09

SHARE WITH EACH OTHER

SCRIPTURE MEMORY

But you are a chosen race, a royal priesthood, a holy nation, a people for his own possession, that you may proclaim the excellencies of him who called you out of darkness into his marvelous light.

—*1 Peter 2:9-10*

LIVING **INTERDEPENDENTLY**

DAY 1

SHARE WHAT YOU CAN SHARE

Scripture Study

ACTS 2:42-47

And they devoted themselves to the apostles' teaching and the fellowship, to the breaking of bread and the prayers. 43 And awe came upon every soul, and many wonders and signs were being done through the apostles. 44 And all who believed were together and had all things in common. 45 And they were selling their possessions and belongings and distributing the proceeds to all, as any had need. 46 And day by day, attending the temple together and breaking bread in their homes, they received their food with glad and generous hearts, 47 praising God and having favor with all the people. And the Lord added to their number day by day those who were being saved.

Observing the Text

What does the text tell us about the specific things the people in the church were doing? How often were these activities occurring?

_____

_____

WEEK 9: SHARE WITH EACH OTHER

What words and phrases are used in the text to describe the people?

_____
_____
_____

What was their attitude toward each other in this season?

_____
_____
_____

Interpreting the Text

The text says, "...all who believed were together and had all things in common." What does the phrase, "all things in common" mean?

_____
_____
_____

Considering the events described, what do you think were the reasons for so many people being saved?

_____
_____
_____

What is significant about the description that they participated in *"the apostles' teaching and the fellowship, to the breaking of bread and the prayers"*?

_____
_____
_____

Teaching

Acts 2:42-47 begins by describing the activities of the most unique group of people ever called together—the church. The church sits under the teaching of the Scripture. The church prays. The church shares in the Lord's Supper. The church enjoys fellowship together. The church baptizes people into the body of Christ. But, another defining characteristic of the church is illustrated in the description given of the very first days of the church: *the church shares*. A gospel family makes provision for needs, sharing food and money and opening their homes. The Bible displays the church as a community of people who care for each other practically and socially.

Think about the faith, the logistics, the practical challenges involved in "selling their possessions and belongings and distributing the proceeds to all, as any had need." People had to be willing to give money away. Someone had to organize collecting the money and distributing it to people. Someone had to figure out who had what needs. And there weren't just a few of these people, but thousands of them.

There is a lot about the scene Luke describes in Acts 2 that makes us want to say "yeah, but..." Yeah, but the apostles were there doing miracles, of course everyone was excited. Yeah, but it was a unique situation that didn't last long. Yeah, but the Bible doesn't say that Christians are supposed to do exactly what the early church did. Yeah, but I can't hang out at church all day, someone has to work to have the money to share.

There is something about this scene that is inspiring and intimidating at the same time. We tend to resist the idea that this might be prescriptive for the church now and not just descriptive of the church then. But, look at the product of all of the teaching and fellowship and sharing and hospitality: "And the Lord added to their number day by day those who were being saved." If the mission of the church is to share the good news of Jesus so that people might be saved, we simply have to pay attention to the model given us in Acts 2. At the heart of this amazing scene is this description of the people: "all who believed were together and had all things in common."

One of the defining characteristics of the church is this radical spiritual and material commonality. You read about it in every book of the New Testament and even in the parts of the Old Testament that describe how God intends for his people to live together. One of the reasons our culture's idols of autonomy and independence are so dangerous is that they undermine the very nature of who God's people are; they are a family, not a group of primarily autonomous individuals.

The beauty of this description of the church in Acts is that it captures a moment when the church was being the church, doing the practical things necessary for a group of individuals to experience and understand what it means to be God's people. It's a winsome picture of true fellowship: "they received their food with glad and generous hearts, praising God and having favor with all the people."

We really can give this gift of unity and generosity to each other. You can make your group into a display of the church that rivals the joy and excitement the first Christians experienced. Share what you have. Open your home. Be hospitable. Teach the Scripture, eat the meals together, pray prayers for each other. It isn't far-fetched at all. It is what God's family does.

LIVING **INTERDEPENDENTLY**

Questions for Reflection

How do you respond to the picture of the church in Acts 2? Why doesn't our church look like that? In what ways does it resemble this picture? Is it really possible? Would you be willing to sell possessions and share with those in need like they did?

What choices would make it possible for your small group to create a community like that in Acts 2?

If your group looked like the Acts 2 community, do you think people would want to participate with you, possibly resulting in their salvation? Why or why not?

Prayer

Ask God to transform you into a catalyst for changing your small group into a community that resembles the church of Acts 2.

SCRIPTURE MEMORY

But you are a _____ race, a royal priesthood, a holy nation, a people for his own possession, that you may _____ the excellencies of him who called you out of darkness into his marvelous light.

—1 Peter 2:9-10

LIVING **INTERDEPENDENTLY**

DAY
2

PLAN TO BE GENEROUS

Scripture Study

ACTS 2:42-47

And they devoted themselves to the apostles' teaching and the fellowship, to the breaking of bread and the prayers. ^{43} And awe came upon every soul, and many wonders and signs were being done through the apostles. ^{44} And all who believed were together and had all things in common. ^{45} And they were selling their possessions and belongings and distributing the proceeds to all, as any had need. ^{46} And day by day, attending the temple together and breaking bread in their homes, they received their food with glad and generous hearts, ^{47} praising God and having favor with all the people. And the Lord added to their number day by day those who were being saved.

EPHESIANS 4:28

Let the thief no longer steal, but rather let him labor, doing honest work with his own hands, so that he may have something to share with anyone in need.

WEEK 9: SHARE WITH EACH OTHER

LEVITICUS 19:9-10

"When you reap the harvest of your land, you shall not reap your field right up to its edge, neither shall you gather the gleanings after your harvest. ¹⁰ And you shall not strip your vineyard bare, neither shall you gather the fallen grapes of your vineyard. You shall leave them for the poor and for the sojourner: I am the Lord your God.

PROVERBS 22:9

Whoever has a bountiful eye will be blessed, for he shares his bread with the poor.

1 CORINTHIANS 16:1-2

Now concerning the collection for the saints: as I directed the churches of Galatia, so you also are to do. ² On the first day of every week, each of you is to put something aside and store it up, as he may prosper, so that there will be no collecting when I come.

Observing the text

What do each of these different texts have in common?

_____
_____
_____

In Proverbs 22:9, why will the person be blessed?

_____
_____
_____

What different groups of people are described in these verses as being recipients of what other people share?

_____
_____

LIVING **INTERDEPENDENTLY**

Interpreting the text

How would having a "bountiful eye" relate to Acts 2:42-47 and also help a person obey the commands in Leviticus 19?

_____
_____
_____

Are the resources being shared in these verses to be given reactively, or are they planned ahead to be shared?

_____
_____
_____

What criteria are given in these texts for who qualifies to be shared with?

_____
_____
_____

Teaching

The Bible is not short on encouraging us with the wisdom of planning ahead. Proverbs 6:6 says, "Go to the ant, O sluggard; consider her ways, and be wise. Without having any chief, officer, or ruler, she prepares her bread in summer and gathers her food in harvest." As far as the Proverb writer is concerned, it is such basic common sense to plan ahead that to not do so is to be less wise than a lowly ant. The comparison is intentionally insulting. No one is making this tiny little ant do what makes sense, she just does it, so what does that say about you if you don't?

Each of the texts we read today calls us to plan ahead. It is the wise thing

WEEK 9: SHARE WITH EACH OTHER

to do, and it is what all good stewards of God do. But, you can see these texts call us to plan ahead not only for our personal provision, but also for the potential needs of others. It is a repeated command of Scripture: set aside for others, don't consume everything you have yourself, and remember the needs of other people when you go to work and when you harvest.

A gospel family shares the burden and responsibility of meeting each other's material needs. The simple reality is that it makes a lot more sense to think, plan ahead, and set aside for the needs we know will eventually emerge. When a tragedy happens or someone loses a job, it is an entirely different experience for everyone involved if each of you has been wise and obedient, like the ant, and prepared ahead of time. If you haven't planned ahead to share, a sudden need is just an added problem to the financial strain already present, and any potential giving is grudging and limited, it isn't enjoyable. But, if you have planned ahead to share, when you have the opportunity to do so you can give with joy and satisfaction that you are serving God and helping your brother or sister; you are using your resources the way God commanded you and the way you planned to use them. It's always rewarding when things go according to plan!

As you consider how you will plan ahead to be generous with the people in your group, consider Proverbs 22:9: "Whoever has a bountiful eye will be blessed, for he shares his bread with the poor." What does it mean to have a "bountiful eye"? It simply means that you trust God's provision for you, so you view the material things you have as sufficient and abundant. The greater your understanding of his provision over even the greatest of your needs, the more "bountiful" your eye. The Bible doesn't quantify this for us, because a bountiful eye is a matter of perspective, not numbers.

LIVING **INTERDEPENDENTLY**

Questions for Reflection

Why do you think the Bible has multiple texts encouraging us to plan ahead to share with others?

_____
_____
_____

Do you set resources aside so that you can help others and be glad about it?

_____
_____
_____

How does this intentional, purposeful generosity bring glory to God?

_____
_____
_____

Would you say you have accepted your responsibility to plan ahead for other's needs, or are you still needing to grow? What will help you begin to obey?

_____
_____
_____

Prayer

Ask God to give you the faith in him and the love for others to set aside some resources now so you can help someone in the future.

SCRIPTURE MEMORY

But you are a chosen race, a royal _____, a holy nation, a people for his own _____, that you may proclaim the excellencies of him who _____ you out of darkness into his marvelous light.

—*1 Peter 2:9-10*

LIVING **INTERDEPENDENTLY**

DAY 3

PEOPLE ARE DIFFERENT

Scripture Study

ACTS 2:42-47

And they devoted themselves to the apostles' teaching and the fellowship, to the breaking of bread and the prayers. [43] And awe came upon every soul, and many wonders and signs were being done through the apostles. [44] And all who believed were together and had all things in common. [45] And they were selling their possessions and belongings and distributing the proceeds to all, as any had need. [46] And day by day, attending the temple together and breaking bread in their homes, they received their food with glad and generous hearts, [47] praising God and having favor with all the people. And the Lord added to their number day by day those who were being saved.

1 CORINTHIANS 12:12-20

For just as the body is one and has many members, and all the members of the body, though many, are one body, so it is with Christ. [13] For in one Spirit we were all baptized into one body—Jews or Greeks, slaves or free—and all were made to drink of one Spirit.

WEEK 9: SHARE WITH EACH OTHER

14 For the body does not consist of one member but of many. 15 If the foot should say, "Because I am not a hand, I do not belong to the body," that would not make it any less a part of the body. 16 And if the ear should say, "Because I am not an eye, I do not belong to the body," that would not make it any less a part of the body. 17 If the whole body were an eye, where would be the sense of hearing? If the whole body were an ear, where would be the sense of smell? 18 But as it is, God arranged the members in the body, each one of them, as he chose. 19 If all were a single member, where would the body be? 20 As it is, there are many parts, yet one body.

Observing the Text

In 1 Corinthians 12:12-20, how many times does Paul use the words "body" and "member"?

_____
_____
_____

According to this text, who arranged the parts of the body?

_____
_____
_____

What does Paul say about the relative importance of the various members of the body?

_____
_____
_____

Interpreting the Text

In what ways does 1 Corinthians 12:12-20 overlap Acts 2:42-47?

_____
_____

LIVING **INTERDEPENDENTLY**

Why is the human body a good metaphor for the church?

_____
_____
_____

Why is it significant that God arranged the members of the body as he chose?

_____
_____
_____

How does 1 Corinthians 12 impact your thoughts about your role in the body of Christ? Do you know what function God has given you?

_____
_____
_____

Teaching

In 1 Corinthians 12 and Romans 12, the apostle Paul uses the metaphor of the human body to describe the church. Both of these texts are part of his teaching about spiritual gifts, but they help us understand much more.

One of the most challenging things about the church is that each of us tends to expect other people to think and do things the way we would. We are challenged when people don't share our passions or interests, and we don't understand why they have so much energy to do things that don't interest us. This tendency is detrimental to the church when we attach spiritual significance to different activities and passions, basing our value of people on those things. When this happens we trust and respect those who think and act like us, but we question the faith or value of those who don't.

If you have been in church for very long, you have probably experienced this. People who have a passion for evangelism can't understand why everyone doesn't share their obviously scriptural desire to share the gospel the way they think it should be shared. People with a high capacity for compassion get frustrated with people who don't have the same desire to be present with hurting people. People who have a high value for organization and structure lose respect for people who instead have a much higher value for relationship. Paul addresses this tension with the Corinthians. In essence he says, "People are different," but he doesn't stop there. Paul says that people are different because God created them differently, and he did it on purpose. And, Paul says, there is a good reason for why God made people the way he did.

A body is made up of different parts doing different things. That is true of a human body and the body of Christ. If every part or every person was the same, there would be no body or church. God blessed his church by creating and calling people who are very different to come together so that all the various functions of the body of Christ can be executed by people with passion and energy for them.

The text points out that "in one Spirit" we are baptized. That is, the same Holy Spirit gives each of us birth into this body and supplies the body both its identity in Christ and nourishment in his Word and presence. It is not an accident that you are part of the body of Christ. God adopted you and added you to his family so you can add your gifts, passions, and abilities to complete its ability to function as God intends. *"God arranged the members in the body, each one of them, as he chose."*

God chose to put you and the other people in your group together for his purpose. Don't just accept that those other people have something to contribute, explore it with them! Celebrate that you don't have to do what they can do that you'd really rather not, and celebrate that God made it that way on purpose.

Some people have financial resources to add to the group, some can cook, some are great hosts, some have repair skills, some have building skills, some are organized, and some like parties. Don't miss that all of these practical differences are God's grace and provision for you, your group, and the church. Don't minimize the value of what you can do versus another because they have more money or they know how to fix cars. Give them their place in the body, and give God thanks that he has provided for your group through all of the various functions he's assembled.

Everyone has something to offer. You build the sense of connection and value for each other as you encourage and celebrate everyone giving and serving the way God created them to give and serve. You belong, and so do they.

Questions for Reflection

How have you seen the metaphor of different parts of a body play out in your group?

_____
_____
_____

Do you thank God that he has made other people differently, giving them different passions and skills than you?

_____
_____
_____

WEEK 9: SHARE WITH EACH OTHER

Do you invest the passions and skills you possess in making the body of the church and of your group function at its best?
_____
_____
_____

Do you celebrate the contributions of others with them?
_____
_____
_____

Prayer

Thank God, by name, for the different people in your group and the ways that their unique gifts add to the functioning of your group.

WEEKLY EXERCISE

APPRECIATE THE VALUE OF
ONE ANOTHER

List the names of the people in your group and write a few words describing the specific, practical things each one does that contribute to the group.

WEEK 9: SHARE WITH EACH OTHER

Get Ready for Group

Write your memorized Scripture.

_____
_____
_____
_____
_____

What observations and interpretations of Scripture were most meaningful to you?

_____
_____
_____
_____
_____

Summarize your key takeaway(s) for this week.

_____
_____
_____
_____
_____

What will you tell the group about the results of your exercise this week?

_____
_____
_____
_____
_____

LIVING **INTERDEPENDENTLY**

How has this week helped you better understand and apply the Spiritual Growth Grid?

_____
_____
_____
_____
_____

	REPENT & BELIEVE		
WHO GOD IS	WHAT GOD DID	WHO WE ARE	WHAT WE DO
KING	CALLED	CITIZENS	LISTEN & OBEY
FATHER	ADOPTED	FAMILY	LOVE & SERVE
SAVIOR	SENT	MISSIONARIES	GO & MULTIPLY

10

BOUND BY GRACE

SCRIPTURE MEMORY

But you are a chosen race, a royal priesthood, a holy nation, a people for his own possession, that you may proclaim the excellencies of him who called you out of darkness into his marvelous light.

—*1 Peter 2:9-10*

LIVING **INTERDEPENDENTLY**

DAY 1

ADOPTION CHANGES US

Scripture Study

GALATIANS 4:1-7

I mean that the heir, as long as he is a child, is no different from a slave, though he is the owner of everything, ² but he is under guardians and managers until the date set by his father. ³ In the same way we also, when we were children, were enslaved to the elementary principles of the world. ⁴ But when the fullness of time had come, God sent forth his Son, born of woman, born under the law, ⁵ to redeem those who were under the law, so that we might receive adoption as sons. ⁶ And because you are sons, God has sent the Spirit of his Son into our hearts, crying, "Abba! Father!" ⁷ So you are no longer a slave, but a son, and if a son, then an heir through God.

Observing the Text
What is the difference between an heir and a slave?

_____

_____

_____

How were we "adopted as sons"?

___

What are the "elementary principles of the world"?

___

Interpreting the Text

What is the significance of our new ability to go to God crying "Abba! Father!"?

___

How do redemption in Christ and adoption as children work together?

___

Teaching

We *Love and Serve* each other because we are a *Family* who have been *Adopted* by *God our Father*. Remember the Spiritual Growth Grid.

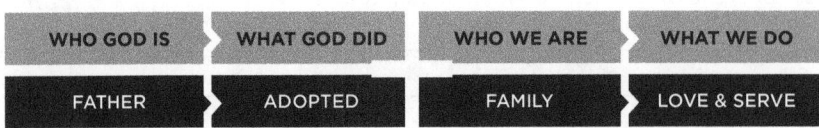

LIVING **INTERDEPENDENTLY**

Adoption changes us. Because of God's love for us, he sent his Son to redeem us from our bondage to sin and the structures and affections of this world. Once we were bound by our sinful nature to be rivals and competitors, focused on our own needs and indifferent to others. But, God made us alive in Christ. He gave us life in his Kingdom and membership in a new family through adoption. You didn't make yourself part of God's family, he chose you and paid the price to redeem you on the cross.

Now you have a true Father. Now you can go to the holy creator of all things and say "Daddy!" You are known and loved, and your adoption guarantees God's protection and provision for you through all eternity.

Adoption changes us. We have a true Father, and we are part of the Father's family. We are a sons, and we are one of many sons.

The studies we have considered for the last nine weeks have focused on the nature of God's family as it relates to living together interdependently. We are to believe in each other and rely on each other. We have examined both the sin barriers to living interdependently and the character traits we receive as God's sons that enable us to be transformed from slaves into sons.

We have been adopted into a new family. We have a new identity, new relationships, and new responsibilities to love and serve the members of our new family in ways that bless and glorify our Father. Let's grow in the ways we honor and serve our new family!

Questions for Reflection
How has having a new identity in Christ changed you?
_____
_____
_____

WEEK 10: BOUND BY GRACE

Are you able to go to God and call him "Daddy"?
_____
_____
_____

Prayer

Give God thanks for adopting you and making you his son!

SCRIPTURE MEMORY

But you are a _____, a royal priesthood, a _____, a people for his own possession, that you may proclaim _____ of him who called you out of darkness into his marvelous light.

—*1 Peter 2:9-10*

LIVING **INTERDEPENDENTLY**

DAY 2

LOVING AND SERVING STRENGTHENS US

Scripture Study

ROMANS 1:8-12

First, I thank my God through Jesus Christ for all of you, because your faith is proclaimed in all the world. ⁹ For God is my witness, whom I serve with my spirit in the gospel of his Son, that without ceasing I mention you ¹⁰ always in my prayers, asking that somehow by God's will I may now at last succeed in coming to you. ¹¹ For I long to see you, that I may impart to you some spiritual gift to strengthen you—¹² that is, that we may be mutually encouraged by each other's faith, both yours and mine.

Observing the text

What does Paul thank God for when he thinks about the church in Rome?

_____
_____
_____

WEEK 10: BOUND BY GRACE

What is the spiritual gift that Paul wants to give and receive from the Romans?

_____
_____
_____

What does Paul do without ceasing?

_____
_____
_____

Interpreting the text

How is another person's faith encouraging? Why would Paul be encouraged by the Romans' faith?

_____
_____
_____

What does this passage in Romans teach us about how we should regard other believers?

_____
_____
_____

Teaching

We *Love and Serve* each other because we are a *Family* who have been *Adopted* by *God our Father*.

In Romans 1:8-12, the apostle Paul says that he longs to be with the Roman church in order to experience the joy of sharing their mutual faith in Jesus. The greatest church planter God ever raised up is strengthened by the shared faith of his brothers and sisters in Christ. Paul could have said he looked forward to celebrating many things in Rome: their obedience, their submission to the authorities, or even the way they handled controversy. But, he wrote that he longs to see them so that they could be mutually encouraged by each other's faith.

As we gather in group each week and interact with each other outside of group, it can be easy to get distracted by our differences in personality, tastes, and spiritual maturity (Paul no doubt had plenty of differences with people in Rome). But don't let that happen. Rather, let us grow in our ability to view each other through the eyes of a fellow follower of Jesus. Let us allow the faith God has given other people to be a source of strength and comfort to us. And let us share our faith energetically, knowing it is a blessing and strength to others.

Paul points out in Romans 3 that we are all sinful, rebellious people who deserve nothing but God's wrath. Yet we are a family because we have received grace and redemption in the broken body and shared blood of Jesus. We are a family because God has united us by our common faith. And we are a family because through our faith in Jesus we are being transformed into his image in unity, mutual submission, and love.

Questions for Reflection
Who do you know personally whose faith encourages you and strengthens your own?

_____
_____
_____

WEEK 10: BOUND BY GRACE

Do you long to see the other people in your group, knowing you will be encouraged by their faith? Do you think that your faith encourages them, so that they long to see you as well?

_____
_____
_____

Prayer

Give thanks for the other members of God's family and the encouragement that their faith brings to you.

SCRIPTURE MEMORY

But you are a chosen race, a _____ _____, a holy nation, a people for his own possession, that you may proclaim the excellencies of him who _____ out of darkness into his marvelous ____.

—*1 Peter 2:9-10*

LIVING **INTERDEPENDENTLY**

DAY
3

FAMILY IS MISSION-CRITICAL

Scripture Study

1 PETER 2:9-10

But you are a chosen race, a royal priesthood, a holy nation, a people for his own possession, that you may proclaim the excellencies of him who called you out of darkness into his marvelous light. [10] Once you were not a people, but now you are God's people; once you had not received mercy, but now you have received mercy.

Observing the Text

Who is the "you" Peter is describing?

_____
_____
_____

What specifically transforms us into God's people?

_____
_____
_____

WEEK 10: BOUND BY GRACE

What purpose is given for God making us into "his people"?

_____

_____

_____

Interpreting the Text

Why is it critical for Christians to understand that they are not autonomous but part of a whole people of God?

_____

_____

_____

How does the way we live together as a family impact how effective we are at proclaiming "the excellencies of him who called you out of darkness into his marvelous light"?

_____

_____

_____

Teaching

We *Love and Serve* each other because we are a *Family* who have been *Adopted* by *God our Father*.

1 Peter 2:9-10 says that being a family is "mission-critical." Peter says that by God's mercy we are a race, a priesthood, a nation—a people created for the specific purpose of declaring to the world the excellencies, mercifulness, and graciousness of God. It would be impossible to overstate the importance of how living out our identity as God's family impacts how well we accomplish this common purpose.

LIVING **INTERDEPENDENTLY**

Think about the implications of this text for how we treat each other. First, Peter says we are a "chosen race." We are all here by God's power and God's choice. When we love and serve one another, we affirm and bless God's decision to include each of us. When we love and serve one another, we worship God and declare his excellencies to the community around us.

We are a "royal priesthood." The purpose of the priesthood is to mediate God's presence to his people and the world. As we love and serve each other, we mediate God's love, patience, kindness, generosity, and grace to each other in a way the world will notice.

We are a "holy nation." We are devoted to God and set apart for God's use. The way we treat each other must affirm what the church says we believe about God's family to the community outside the church.

We are a "people for God's own possession." We are not controlled by the ways of the world but seek to live as children of our Father. We are set apart by honoring God's values and reflecting God's character to each other. People will be attracted to the church because of the difference that grace makes in our relationships.

May we live lives that are worthy of our identity in Christ! We are a family. We are a chosen race. We are a royal priesthood. We are a holy nation. We are God's own people.

Questions for Reflection

How accurately does your life reflect your true identity as a member of God's family—chosen race, royal priesthood, holy nation, God's own possession?

_____
_____
_____

WEEK 10: BOUND BY GRACE

How thoroughly does our identity show up in your group?
_____
_____
_____

Prayer

Ask God to accomplish his purpose in the world through how well you reflect the new identity he has given you as part of his chosen race. Pray that he would enable you to walk in the reality of your identity as his adopted child.

WEEKLY EXERCISE

HOW DID WE GROW?

Reflect on the last nine weeks study on "Living Interdependently."

List:

- The most spiritually challenging part of the study for you.
- One area where you have grown through the study.
- One way you are behaving differently as a result of this study.

Get Ready for Group

Write your memorized Scripture.
_____
_____
_____
_____
_____

What observations and interpretations of Scripture were most meaningful to you?
_____
_____
_____
_____
_____

Summarize your key takeaway(s) for this week.
_____
_____
_____
_____
_____

What will you tell the group about the results of your exercise this week?
_____
_____
_____
_____
_____

LIVING **INTERDEPENDENTLY**

How has this week helped you better understand and apply the Spiritual Growth Grid?

_____
_____
_____
_____
_____

REPENT & BELIEVE

WHO GOD IS	WHAT GOD DID	WHO WE ARE	WHAT WE DO
KING	CALLED	CITIZENS	LISTEN & OBEY
FATHER	ADOPTED	FAMILY	LOVE & SERVE
SAVIOR	SENT	MISSIONARIES	GO & MULTIPLY

www.ingramcontent.com/pod-product-compliance
Lightning Source LLC
Chambersburg PA
CBHW070140100426
42743CB00013B/2779